The Selected Works of R. Page Arnot
First Prism Key Press Edition 2012

Prism Key Press
New York, NY 10001
PrismKeyPress.com

ISBN-13: 978-1481130394

The Selected Works of R. Page Arnot

Contents

Unemployment

The men that worked for England,
They have their graves at home;
And bees and birds of England,
About the cross can roam.

But they that fought for England,
Followed a falling star,
Alas, alas, for England,
They have their graves afar.

And they that rule in England,
In stately conclave met.
Alas, alas, for England,
They have no grave as yet.

—G. K. Chesterton.

Last week and the week before were full of surface excitements. British soldiers were ambushed in Ireland, well-known Irishmen were thrown into gaol, warehouses were fired in Liverpool, the Houses of Parliament were closed to the public, and barricades were put up in Downing Street. The newspapers are alternately depressed and excited. Ministers of the Crown are reported to be full of activity, and everything is done to frighten the good inhabitants of Kensington into a wholehearted support of the Government. But beneath all this there is a good reason for Cabinet Ministers to display the anxious activity with which they are credited by the newspapers. From behind the barricades they are peering out at something more dreadful than their Sinn Fein adversaries, something before which their political witchcraft and their armed forces are to no avail. They do not face it or understand what it is: they refer to it as "bad trade," or "period of depression," or "heavy unemployment figures." They dare not realise what is actually upon them, even to themselves they dare not say: *"Capitalist production is ceasing to produce."*

Pills for an Earthquake

Meantime, they are busied with hasty attempts to mitigate the crisis. Out-of-work benefit is being paid at the miserable rate of 15s. a week. Arterial roads are to be constructed. Schemes of relief are to be encouraged. But the Government is well aware that whatever they may do now will only have a surface effect. To go deeper they dare not; for the only remedy for this mortal sickness of society would mean the destruction of all they are trying to preserve.

Bourbons of Industry

The employers, for their part, speaking through their mouthpiece, the Federation of British Industries, have issued their pronouncement. For two years now they have been calling for "More production." And now, by this winter, every worker knows that by "more production" is meant, not production for use, not for cheapening of goods, but such a greater output per man as will reduce the "labour cost" of every job and gain for the employer a greater profit or wider markets. The worker knows now that though the employer may call it "production" in his speeches, he writes it down as "profit" in his books. Yet the F.B.I., having learnt nothing, is still calling for "More Production."

The End of Devil Worship

Faced by this, and remembering the calls that were made on him during the war; remembering, too, his relatives and his friends who were killed to make the world safe for democracy, the worker is beginning to awaken to the nature of capitalism. For too long he has been drugged. It is now with him as it was in the maritime empire of Carthage. We read that the

8

Carthaginians used to feed their god Moloch with human sacrifices. But the victims were drugged before their bodies were thrust into the furnaces, so that the men and women who were passing their children through the fire to Moloch heard no cries that might disturb their besotted adoration of their god. But now the victims are undrugged; their shrieks are heard and the listening crowd of worshippers of capitalist efficiency and sufficiency are beginning to wonder. The masses of workers are beginning in their minds already to make an end of the cruel deity.

The Attack on the Workers

While the workers are thus awakening, the employing class and its Government behind all their concern for reconstruction, for mitigations, for "solutions of the problem of unemployment" are deeply roused to defend themselves. In Parliament we have Bills, and at banquets we have speeches; throughout the country we have the apparatus for doling out the fifteen shillings. All over Europe we have the same ostensible concern. In Germany, in France, in Italy, this crisis is found and for it these sticking-plasters are made. But beneath all this something impels the capitalists to work for their own ruin. Those that are doomed go mad before their end. And so the successful robbers of Versailles and the penitent thieves of the Wilhelmstrasse alike are prepared to use the crisis for a desperate attack on the working class.

The New "Economists"

In this country the cry is "economy." Everything is to be "cut down." What is everything? Is it to be the Navy, the armies of Mesopotamia and India, the garrison of Ireland, the luxuries of the rich, their mansions and motor cars, their fashionable and expensive doctors, their Public Schools and private tutors? No. No. What is to be "cut down" is the worker's education, the worker's housing, the hospitals for the workers. Of all these aids to his standard of life the worker is to be deprived; the working women and children are to work double shift in the factories, and "above all, wages are to be cut down. And should a Communist make a speech which might be dangerous to these "economists," then that man too must be cut down.

It is the same as it was a hundred years ago, after Waterloo. Again we have a world shattered by war, markets impoverished abroad and misery and oppression at home. And every month the capitalists are proving themselves essentially the same as they were in the time of Sidmouth and Castlereagh. Only this time the working class are organised to protect themselves against capitalism, and, it may be, soon to overthrow it.

The Crisis of Capitalism

The situation is, therefore, this: The after war crisis of which unemployment is a part, is finding no solution in the measures of the Government. On the contrary, the crisis is awakening the workers to the nature of capitalism, and at the same time is rousing the capitalist forces to deliver an attack on the working class. The counter-attack of the workers is not the seizing of town halls and libraries by the men out-of-work. Not even if they go further and seize factories will it be the counter-attack. The real counter to the onslaught of the capitalist's lies in the feeling of the workers that they have a moral right to do things that are "illegal" and "criminal." The spirit of the workers is rising superior to the morality imposed on them by capitalism. The man lacking bread to give to his wife and children is a terrible figure which towers above the puny morality and legality of capitalism, and demands in a voice of thunder the reason for capitalism's existence. To that annihilating question capitalism has no reply. It has sunk into moral disrepute. It is rejected and despised, and its end is near. *Capitalist production is ceasing to produce.*

What is the immediate task for the worker? The measure of defence afforded him by his trade unions will not last for many months. The trade union funds accumulated during the full employment period of the war will be drained away more rapidly than in 1908-9, when the cost of administration was a bagatelle compared to what it is now. In many industries at present the capitalists would welcome the prospect of a strike, and the current demands for reduction in wages are not trade by them in any forgetfulness of this fact. If then at the end of some months the worker finds himself with his back to the wall, what is he to do? There is nothing but to fight in an ever sterner mood; to recast organisation of his trade unions into a more effective formation; to base the unit of organisation on the unit of production, and, snatching courage from despair, to join together with his fellow workers in industrial unions. The mood of despair does not last. It passes from despair into desperation, and when that point is reached nothing can hold from massing together for the overthrow of a civilisation that is decayed and rotting

Book Review: A Russian Philippic

The Defence of Terrorism: **(Terrorism and Communism): A Reply to Karl Kautsky, by L. Trotsky.**
Preface by H.N. Brailsford
The Labour Publishing Company, Ltd., London
3s. 6d.

"TERRORISM AND COMMUNISM" was written sixteen months ago, in the midst of the Russo-Polish war. It is a strange spectacle to see a Minister for War, in the midst of a military crisis, engaged in a bookish controversy. But the explanation is not difficult. The whole driving force of the revolution depends on the belief of the Bolshevik theorists that they have been and are theoretically right and that the other Socialist theorists are wrong. Now of the other Socialist theorists by far the best known on the Continent is Karl Kautsky. For many years he was the High Priest of Marxism, and from the editorial chair of *Die Neue Zeit* spoke as *ex cathedra.* He was considered the orthodox exponent of Marxism, and many a working man learned his theoretic Socialism from his book on the Erfurt Programme. For the Bolsheviks it is, therefore, of great importance to show that at any rate the later utterances of Kautsky are an abandonment of the correct Marxist position. Another reason is furnished by Trotsky himself in his introduction, when he answers the question, "Is it still necessary to refute Kautsky theoretically?"

It may be said that the will of the working masses of the whole of the civilised world, directly influenced by the course of events, is at the present moment incomparably more revolutionary than their consciousness, which is still dominated by the prejudices of parliamentarism and compromise. The struggle for the dictatorship of the working class means, at the present moment, an embittered struggle with Kautskianism within the working class. .... This book must serve the ends of an irreconcilable struggle against the cowardice, half-measures, and hypocrisy of Kautskianism in all countries.

The effect of this reply, however, goes far beyond any mere purpose of answering Kautsky. Indeed, in future Kautsky may be remembered only for his having provoked one of the most brilliant pieces of polemical writing in Socialist history. This book is written in the grand style: and, whichever way it is judged, will keep a place amongst the masterpieces of political argument.

The book answers Kautsky, it is true, but not in the somewhat plodding way, which makes such heavy reading, of Marx's "Philosophy of Poverty" or Lenin's "Proletarian Revolution." Trotsky himself generates the necessary excitement by the bravura of his style for appreciating the intensity of the fight and for understanding the sword-play. Marx here and there turns from the analysis of the errors of Proudhon to a statement of the correct view-point: Trotsky turns from the sweep of his enunciation of the correct view-point to deal with the errors of Kautsky.

He deals first with "the balance of power," then turns to the dictatorship of the proletariat. Here, more than once, there suddenly emerges the scorn of the practical man who is also a theorist (the Philosopher-King) for the philosopher who has never had to apply his theories. For Kautsky, reliance on persuasion is the best weapon of the proletariat. Trotsky rallies him, asking brutally:—

Is it possible that Kautsky is leaning to the idea that the bourgeoisie can be held down with the help of the categorical imperative, which in his last writings plays the part of the Holy Ghost? . . . Every White Guard has long ago acquired the simple truth that it is easier to hang a Communist to a branch of a tree than to convert him with a book of Kautsky's. These gentlemen have no superstitious fear, either of the principles of democracy or of the flames of hell.

He leaves it at that and the argument proceeds with the most brilliant chapter in the book, the chapter on "Democracy." The chapter on "Terrorism" deals with all the revolutions of modern history up to and including the time of the Bolsheviks, up to the time of the revolutionary terrorism in Russia. The German savant's comparison of the Paris Commune with Soviet Russia is traversed in a closely-reasoned chapter which shows a full knowledge of that episode in proletarian history. Thereafter in the chapters entitled "The Working Class and its Soviet Policy" and "Problems of the Organisation of Labour," Trotsky achieves a miracle of compression and propaganda. Within its compass it is probably the best short statement and defeat of Soviet Russia that has yet been written. The temper and tone of it suggest a man turning aside from the highest and most exacting form of administrative work to write, not with a tired brain, but a mind at concert pitch. In short, Trotsky is in "top form." At times he rises into a gaiety of invective, of which one example must be reproduced:—

In this connection, Kautsky asks: "Would Trotsky undertake to get on a locomotive and set it going, in the conviction that he would, during the journey, have time to learn and to arrange everything? One must preliminarily have acquired the qualities necessary to drive a locomotive before deciding to set it going. Similarly the proletariat ought beforehand to have acquired those necessary qualities which make it capable of administering industry, once it had taken it over." This instructive comparison would have done honour to any villiage clergyman. None the less, it is stupid. With infinitely more foundation one could say: "Will Kautsky dare to mount a horse before he has learned to sit firmly in the saddle, and to guide the animal its steps?" We have foundations for believing that Kautsky would not make up his mind to such a dangerous purely Bolshevik experiment. On the other hand, we fear that, through not risking to mount the horse, Kautsky would have considerable difficulty in learning the secrets of riding on horseback. For the fundamental Bolshevik prejudice precisely this: that one learns to ride on horseback only when sitting on the horse.

This book, with its well-proportioned argument and its turns of phrase affords a literary pleasure not provided for in the usual Bolshevik literature. But to many readers there is another pleasure in the reading of it, in that it recalls a memory of the great controversies of the past. Surely the situation is unparalleled in the last two hundred years, that a new order of society, challenged to defend itself against the hostility of other nations, should also have to justify its existence on a European forum. For any parallel we have to go back to John Milton's "Defensio pro Populo Anglicano." The translation, as is obvious from the extracts I have quoted, is singularly well done, a thing for which we have reason to be grateful, particularly in translations from the Russian. The English is vivid and easy. There is, so far as I have noticed, only one mistake—in the passage where the Russian "Subbota" is given its normal translation "Saturday" instead of, as it should be in this particular place, "the Sabbath." The printing is also good. But this praise for the auxiliaries of an author cannot be extended to the publishers, at least one respect. The change of the original title "Terrorism and Communism" to "The Defence of Terrorism" seems likely to be confusing to the bibliographer in the future, and positively misleading as to the contents of the book.

R. P. A.

16

Book Review: A Second Writing on the Wall

Red Revolt: The Rand Strike
January-March, 1922.
By S.P. Bunting.
Communist Party of South Africa.
1s. 6d.

Before the war a remarkable thing happened in the British Empire. That curious political unit, with its variegated list of constitutions and forms of government, was characterised throughout, we were told, by certain uniform principles of administration. These principles were difficult to define in such a way as to mark them off clearly from the principles upon which the French or German empires were conducted: but it was always understood that the British principles were quite distinctive. For instance, it was usual to say that the British Empire was distinguished from all others by the Rule of Law, by the strict adherence of each and every authority to the traditional charters of the English race, by the jealous safeguarding of the liberty of the subject. The old Freedom of the Germanic mark, the independence that was born in the Hercynian forest, was preserved on the banks of the Limpopo, amongst the Antipodes, and generally wherever the Union Jack was flown. But above all it was in the dominions overseas that the ideals of Liberty, Democracy, and even-handed Justice were understood to have their greatest practical realisation. In this earthly paradise there happened before the war, as I have said, a remarkable thing.

On the banks of the Limpopo, in February, 1914, Magna Carta, Habeas Corpus, and many other venerable parchments were suddenly torn across. There had been a general strike. It was quelled by the arbitrary arrest of the strike leaders (Habeas Corpus torn) and, without trial of any kind (Magna Carta torn), by their expulsion from the Union of South Africa. The sailing of the steamship *Umgeni* with the deportees on board could not be countermanded by any fiat of the Colonial Office, which courteously lamented its inability in the matter in answer to the expostulations of the Labour members. The class struggle had reached an acute stage, and forthwith the class governing in South Africa jettisoned the whole bourgeois cargo of ideals. The effect was profound and immediate. Everywhere throughout the British Empire, on both sides of the class struggle, the eyes of the young men were opened.

In the face of this event in South Africa the astonished cackle about the Bolsheviks and their view that the governing class, when put to it, would behave similarly in every country is ridiculous. The lesson that the safety of the governing class over-rode all other considerations (of law, liberty, justice, &c.) could be learned, and was learned, long before the Bolsheviks were ever heard of. How comes it, nevertheless, that the lesson was not universally learned? Was it possible that the union leaders and the chief Socialists in this country drew no conclusions whatever from this startling reversal of ordered British progress? In some cases, perhaps, this was so. But in many cases the conclusion drawn must have been that the South African affair was something isolated, something exceptional and unrelated in any way to the general trend of historical development, something (like the war afterwards) that would never happen again.

Not only did it happen again: but it happened under the regime of General Jan Smuts, for whom the Liberals had built a tabernacle, by whose wisdom and reputation for just-dealing the British Cabinet were guided in the last days of the war and the crucial moments of the peace. It was at his eminently Liberal suggestion, we were told, that the idea of an Irish Free State was born. Yet exactly the same thing has taken place under the soulful Smuts as occurred under the brutal Botha. To some this will be the second writing on the wall: but to others it will simply be another "exceptional occurrence." Even to some Labour people it will seem impossible that a nice, kind man like General Smuts could be responsible for anything detrimental to the working class: and rather than believe evil of him they will credulously swallow the Reuter lie which told of documents proving a Bolshevik plot—which documents have never been discovered. Smuts will retain his tabernacle.

Meantime the details of the second demonstration of capitalist dictatorship in South Africa can be read in this useful little booklet by S. P. Bunting.

R.P.A.

The Anti-Communist International

THE Conference at Hamburg in the last week of May, which the Second International and the Vienna Union (or Two-and-a-half International) were fused into a single body, is of great importance in the development of the working-class struggle. It is of importance, but not for the reason given by the fusionists. To them Hamburg is the ending of the divisions in the Socialist movement caused by the great war; to us it marks the formation of a definitely anti-Communist *bloc*, the clearing away of the confusions caused by the wavering centre parties, the paving of the way for fascism in every country.

By all accounts, this Hamburg Conference was very touching. Emotion was generated in great quantities. The leaders of the Second International, long ago forgetting the quarrels they had had as patriotic supporters of the Kaiser on the one hand, and of the Entente bourgeoisie on the other, had been sorely vexed by the revolt of their pacifist sections during and immediately after the war. The faith of Clifford Allen in the wise leadership of Henderson had been badly shaken: the faith of Hilferding in Noske had almost entirely disappeared. But now the Second International could use the words of Shakespeare, and say magnanimously of Hamburg that it did "unthread the rude eye of rebellion and welcome home again discarded faith." On its side the Vienna Union, rising to even greater heights of magnanimity was prepared to welcome out of the abundance of its pacifism those who had driven the workers by millions to be killed. The Holy Spirit moved on the face of the waters of the Alster [the river of Hamburg], and everybody was forgiven by everybody else until seventy times seven: there was complete tolerance.

Nevertheless this complete tolerance was rather like the complete religious toleration accorded by Cromwell's Puritans to all religions—"except atheists and Catholics." In the same

21

way the complete tolerance of the Hamburg Conference does not apply to the Communists, and the rules of the new organisation have been very carefully drafted so as to secure that they shall never be applicable to Communists.

The differences which divided the pacifists and the Second International were only apparent: the real difference was between the Communist International and all the others. Thus, the significance of this Hamburg Conference is its formation of a definitely anti-Communist International: everything else is mere words.

The account of the sessions of the Conference and the preliminaries bears this out. First the conditions of summons were such as to exclude the Communists. Only those Parties were invited to attend which accepted the following conditions:

(1) The principle of the economic emancipation of the workers from capitalist domination as their object, and the independent political and industrial section of the workers' organisations as the means of realising that object;

(2) The unity of the International Trade Union movement of Amsterdam as an absolute essential for the realisation of that emancipation;

(3) The resolution of the Hague World Peace Conference, 1922, on "The Mission of organised Labour in the movement of World Peace," as the present basis in all action when there is imminent danger of war, and recognise the necessity of adopting a clear and definite policy to be pursued by the workers' movement in case of war;

(4) Recognise the Labour and Socialist International, not only as an effective instrument in peace, but an absolute essential during war;

(5) Agree after the formation of a Labour and Socialist International not to affiliate to any other political International.

Clause 1 means anything or nothing. Clause 4 is the sort of death-bed repentance that pleases priests; as the song goes, "When the devil was ill, the devil a monk would be." Clauses 2 and 5 are directed against the Communist International, and in so far as a reference in Clause 3 to the farcical Hague Conference of last year has any meaning at all, it is to debar the Bolsheviks because they will not stop exposing it as a farce. Not only were the pre-conditions of the Conference thus mainly aimed at the Communists, but out of all the discussions the one that was marked by a note of passionate sincerity was that in which the Communists were cursed, damned, and excommunicated. It is impossible, reading the fragmentary accounts of the Conference, not to be struck by the whole-hearted sincerity of the hatred shown to the Communist International. It contrasts with the insincerity of the fundamental paragraph of the new Constitution, which is as follows:

"The Labour and Socialist International (L.S.I.) is a union of such parties as accept the principle of the class struggle for the economic emancipation of the workers from capitalist domination and the establishment of the Socialist Commonwealth as their object, and the independent political and industrial action of the workers' organisations as a means of realising that object."

"Such parties as accept the principle of the class struggle." How does this square with the repeated declarations of the Labour Party that it is not a class party, or with the repudiations of Marxism by its best known leaders? In its total

23

abstention from the class struggle at home, and its swallowing the formula of the class struggle during its week-end at Hamburg the Labour Party is like some Scotch teetotallers of my acquaintance, who, when at home in Glasgow "Never touched it," but were perfectly willing to tipple at Brodick Fair. The significance of this Hamburg Conference, then, emerges in its anti-Communist character. But to have said that is not an explanation. It is necessary to discover how it should be anti-Communist, how the many divisions in the Labour movement have gradually disappeared or been stopped up, leaving the one big gulf between the Communists and the anti-Communists.

To get this, we must go a little further back than the emergence of the Vienna Union. The question is that of the most fundamental division first showing itself in debate, and secondly in Party organisation. It is the difference between those who believe in co-operation, however partial, however temporary, but still co-operation, with the bourgeois State and those who will have nothing to do with the capitalist State. That difference emerged at the International Socialist Congress held at Amsterdam in 1904. A well-known French socialist had taken part in the formation of a French radical cabinet. He claimed that his action was perfectly consistent with a socialist standpoint, or (since the word Socialist is now used to justify any and every activity) let us put it that he frankly endeavoured to justify his action on the ground that it was in the true interests of the proletariat. The matter was debated in France in 1903; it was brought up at the International Socialist Congress in 1904. Jaures, Bebel, Kautsky and all the others discussed it, and in the end it was decided that the action of that French socialist was opposed to the interests of the working class. The name of that French Socialist was Alexandre Millerand: he is now head of the capitalist State in France.

Further, it was laid down that no socialist must enter a coalition with the bourgeois parties. But the decision went deeper than the mere question of joining this or that ministry. It was the division between those who believed in working with

24

the capitalist state and those who, believing the State to be the Executive Committee of the capitalist class, would have no truck with it. It is true that the poison within the Second International was even then at work, the poison which consisted in adding clause after clause to resolutions until they became perfectly meaningless, and so could not possibly offend anyone. Therefore this decision was hedged about with clauses which allowed for exceptions, but the actual decision does not matter: the important thing is that the two fundamentally conflicting conceptions of socialism were brought to an issue.

It was therefore but as a pendant to this resolution on working class independence that the Congresses of Stuttgart (1907), Copenhagen (1910), and Basle (1912) passed and repassed the resolutions defining the attitude of the Socialist parties in the case of a European war. The outbreak of the war, however, concealed for a time the fundamental differences. The line of cleavage was between those who supported their Governments, making timely use of the exceptional clauses in the 1904 resolution in order to enter coalitions, become ministers and effective recruiting agents on the one side, and on the other those who being tinged with Cobdenite pacifism would not support their Government in a war, together, of course, with the minority who remained faithful to the resolutions of the International capitalist resolution and would have no truck with the bourgeois on any action. The lines of division occurring in this manner it was some little time before the true differences began to appear. At the Zimmerwald Conference of September, 1915, the cry was not for peace through socialism and social revolution, but simply for peace, peace without annexations and without indemnities, peace at once and peace at any price. The succeeding Conference of anti-war socialists held in April, 1916, at Kienthal made the distinction plain. The language of the resolutions is clear. Not only are the patriotic socialists denounced, but the futility of bourgeois pacifism is exposed, and the hope of any real peace under capitalism is declared to be an illusion; the only peace that endures will come with the triumph of socialism. The triumph of socialism is, therefore, the only urgent question.

Already we see the outlines of the Third International gleaming; already the complete betrayal of the workers by the chiefs of the Second International has made it clear that the new International, if it is to start clean and honest must not include any of these discredited traders and bankrupt merchants.

At the same time as the Versailles Conference, a Socialist Conference is held at Basle: that Conference is like the marionette players. The Entente Socialists raise the question of Germany 's guilt at the same time as Monsieur Clemenceau and others are reaching, on the same subject at Versailles, and the German Social Democratic Party replies to the same purpose as, a few months later, did Count Brockdorff Rantzau at Versailles. In the best manner of the Big Four dictating to the defeated Central Empires, it was laid down that future congresses should have as a main item on their agenda the question of the responsibility for the war; the second main item which it was decided should be discussed was the question of Democracy. A resolution was passed which contained the telling phrase:

> "A society more and more permeated with socialism (the Fabian touch) cannot be realised, much less permanently established, unless it rests upon triumphs of DEMOCRACY and has rooted in the principles of liberty."

We are back again it is clear to the year 1776, and the American Declaration of Independence that preceded and guaranteed the white terrors of capitalism of the United States. To the resolution on Democracy the answer was given in the next month, March, 1919, in the "Thesis on Bourgeois Democracy and Proletarian Dictatorship," the first pronouncement of the newly-formed Communist International.

The ambiguities of the pre-war International were past; the possibility of contradictory views existing in the same organisation no longer survived: it had led to the bloodshed of 1914. Against those who had insisted on fulfilling the 1904 resolution against co-operation with the bourgeoisie, there was uttered the shibboleth of Democracy and liberty by the war-mongers, who (to do them justice), never failed to say that it was for these things they were fighting or inducing others to fight. The challenge was taken up, and the nature of bourgeois democracy and bogus liberty, examined and exposed. It is no wonder that the jingo Socialists have now formed an anti-Communist International.

The call of the Third International was at once responded to. Movement was felt amongst the workers, everywhere the leaders were forced to make the appearance of a move towards the new International. Inside such parties as the French Socialist Party, the German Independent Socialist Party, the I.L.P., the response of the working class elements was unmistakable. The leaders, however, hesitated. They stated that they were anxious to have a reconstructed international on a wider basis than that laid down in the Manifesto of the Third International. They wanted something, as the I. L. P. put it, which would leave the national sections complete autonomy, by which I understand it meant liberty to accept the class-struggle in international congresses and to repudiate it at home. In Germany, in France, and in other countries during the next eighteen months the majority of the parties, including nearly all the working class elements, went over to the Communist International.

It might have been thought that the adherence of the majority of these parties to the Communist International settled the question. No, curiously enough, it was immediately after the adhesion of the majority of these parties that the remainder set themselves to build up an International which would neither be the Second International nor the Third International, and which approximately received the name of the Two-and-a-Half. Before they began it was predicted that they were a sort of astral body, temporarily detached from the Second International, and that while this astral body might roam for a time through the ether in quest of its ideal of cosmic unity, it was bound sooner or later to return to the *vile corpus*, from which it was but an emanation. They carried on this spiritualistic trickery for a couple of years, at the end of which, they suddenly re-united with the jingo Socialists, crying as they did so, "At last we have the one united International."

No doubt some of them really deceived themselves. Socialists brought up in the atmosphere of Imperialistic Britain are naturally adepts at the art of self-deception. One can imagine Charles Buxton, or better still, Clifford Allen, as Sir Galahad in search of the Holy Grail of International Unity. Again and again they cross the misty seas, again and again they return defeated, but still hopeful. At last one fine May-day, in the year of our Saviour nineteen-hundred-and-twenty-three, they come sailing over the sea from Germany and spread the glad tidings that they have found the Holy Grail: and the faith and fervour of Sir Galahad is so strong that no one has the courage to break it to him that what he has got is not the Holy Grail of Joseph of Arimathea, but simply a batterered old pint pot from the tavern of the Second International.

The object of spiritualists, like other charlatans, is to fool the populace, and holy legends, like that of Sir Galahad, have often bemused a people in the past and helped to keep it from revolt. Here it is that we find the reason for the existence of the Two-and-a-Half. After the war, within a few short months, as the workers began to realise their conditions, the chiefs of the Second International with their policies and reformist illusions, were hopelessly discredited. For nearly three years after the armistice the masses were still in a revolutionary mood. What is more, that mood was growing and spreading ever wider. At the beginning large numbers of the workers were sunk in slumber, lulled by the promises of the Second International, made when they were members of Governments and Royal Ministers; with the end of the war, and even before it in some cases, the trustfulness of the masses passed away. Very quickly it became clear that nothing would hold them back from following a revolutionary lead, or at any rate, from following those who spoke in revolutionary phrases, whether they meant it or not. The old magics were stale: reformism was seen through as an illusion: the overthrow of capitalism was recognised as the only solution that would be lasting. It was at this point that the Centre Parties, the Parties whose leaders afterwards formed the Two-and-a-Half, began to talk wild, began to pass most revolutionary resolutions, began to invent special red pigments and paint themselves all over. The German Independent Socialists in December, 1919, at their Leipsig Congress, declared for Workers' Councils and also for the dictatorship of the proletariat. It was all camouflage, of course, but the workers were not to know that. Nothing could be more scathing than the references of some of the Two-and-a-Half people to the Second International. They referred to it with opprobrious epithets, and even as late as December, 1920, the manifesto of the preliminary meeting of the Two-and-a-Half referred to the "so called Second International" as the "only obstacle to the unity of the working class." More than that, the I.L.P. set about revising its obsolete constitution, and in proof of its modernity called in Mr. G. D. H. Cole to help. The months from the signature of the Versailles Treaty to the spring of 1922 were passed in the most desperate and revolutionary manner. Swashbuckling speeches were made by the Centrists, and in return for the swashbuckling speeches the bourgeois Governments handed out some transient concessions. The working class, or parts of it, stilled by these concessions, rejoiced that they had followed the tactics of the Two-and-a-Half and not run after the men of Moscow, who were so dangerous, so divorced from common sense, so unaware of political conditions in this country (whichever country it was), so narrow in their views.

When the tide turned, when the capitalist offensive

begun, their work was finished. First their tone changed into one of much greater conciliation; secondly, the concessions they had won were taken away again by the capitalists (for example, Trade Boards Extension, Mines Act, etc.); and finally, under the stress of the capitalist offensive, the revolutionary mood of the workers and the concessions that bought off that revolutionary mood having both disappeared, the Two-and-a-Half International quietly disappeared also. It was gathered to its forefathers, its forefathers of the Second International. Deceiving or self-deceived (it does not greatly matter which) it had served the capitalists in their hour of need. This was the historic rôle of the Two-and-a-Half International.

But the importance of the recent Conference was not so much in its Organisation of the anti-Communist forces within the working class as such, or in the fitting ending that it gave to the meteoric career of the Two-and-a-half, but in its relation to the menace of the capitalist offensive. It is by its alteration of the factors in the class struggle that the Hamburg Conference is really important.

Let us for a moment consider the position of the enemy. The Bourgeoisie, like the socialists of the Second International, has for five long years hoped for normalcy, for tranquility, for a return of the good old peaceful days and so on. Every disturbance, every uprising, everything that would tell an experienced observer that he was on the verge of a volcano, tells them simply nothing. All these things are so many isolated instances, and to none more so than to the journalists and pundits of the new Labour and Socialist International. "If only Monsieur Poincaré were defeated," they sigh, or, "If only the President of the U.S.A. would authorise a billion credits to Europe," or, "Now that Mr. Lloyd George has gone, if only Lord Robert Cecil would"—; so they go on. But after five years of these hopes, some amongst the bourgeoisie are beginning to doubt if the world can be set right so easily. The times are rather out of joint, they feel, and drastic must be the remedy. They find on the one hand an anarchy of production which has led to the crisis of unemployment that continually threatens future wars, struggles for the markets and "yards of mud between two blades of grass." Against this they have no remedy. Their spells and incantations, their armed forces and their aeroplane squadrons, their hoarded gold and their printing presses are all of no avail. On the other hand they feel that their trouble comes from the movements and uneasy stirring of the subject classes against them. If the weapons of persuasion, religious dope, class education and newspaper propaganda have no effect, then repression must be used. Is not repression used already? it may be asked. Indeed it is, but legal repression in these days is not enough. The learned professors read in their books that the repressive laws of the Spartans against their Helots were not enough to ensure the safety of the State, and that therefore divers of the Lacedeamonian young men were licensed to walk abroad and put to death any Helot they might find. A lesson like that can be very easily applied: and Fascism is the result. It has begun in Italy; it has spread to Poland and Hungary and Yugo-Slavia; there are signs of it in France, and it has its backers in this country. It has sprung up in various forms in America, and even in Japan, where there might seem but little need of it—so complete is the domination of the ruling class. It has begun. Before the next election in France, Fascism will be tried, while the whole policy of the Entente towards Germany is to destroy the "Jew Republic," as they call it, and introduce a monarchist, Fascist, re-action to seize power. Exit the new German State and the pale shadow of socialisation, of which the Second International was once so proud.

As Fascism spreads, everything gets ready for a grand final assault on Soviet Russia. Even as I write, the news comes through that sixty Japanese Communists have been arrested on a charge of "conspiring to set up a Communist Party." As Marcel Cachin was arrested by the Ruhr-monger Poincaré, so the arrest of these Japanese Communists will be utilised to prevent a Trade Agreement between Japan and Soviet Russia. The European situation is black; the world situation is blacker still.

The formation of the Labour and Socialist International paves the way to Fascism. Firearms Acts may be put in force against the workers: nothing disarms the workers so completely or heartens the would-be Fascists so much as the Labour and Socialist International. Do we see any sign of it in this country? The answer is in the affirmative. In the spring of this year there was every sign of a Labour revolt. The mood of despair amongst the workers was passing away. *The Times*, which knows its England, was saying gloomily that the country was in far the biggest industrial struggles it had ever faced. The builders, the agricultural workers, the miners, the shipbuilders, all these, and many more, were on the move. Where is that revolt now, what has smothered it? Everyone has forgotten the gloomy anticipations of the governing class, and what has smothered it? It was the combination of the Labour machine with the bourgeois machine: the sleeper was awakening, everything had to be done to keep him quiet. Thus, while Fascism is being prepared behind the scenes the stage is set for Fascism by the complete organisation of the Labour forces of Western Europe under the constitutionalist banner. It effectually does disarm the, workers. Apart from those led by the Communists, the workers put-up no resistance, physical or moral. When the British Mussolini is given his cue and steps on to the stage, he will be able to say that it was "a bloodless revolution."

Book Review: Real "Economic Science"

A Short Course of Economic Science, by A. Bogdanoff.
Tanslated: J. Fineberg.
391 pp.
Labour Publishing Company

THERE is a remarkable contrast in this country between the eager desire of the workers to be filled with a knowledge of the basic process of society—essentially an instinct to understand their exploitation, and to get rid of it—and the awful sawdust of "economics" with which they are stuffed. Educational class after educational class turns away from the allurements of studying "literature," or "architecture," or "the history of art," or any other of the university pastimes, and demands instead an understanding of "economics," or "economic history," or "economic geography," or "industrial history." For under one or other of these labels they hope to find the thing they want. What do they get? In each case they get, not what they want, but a narrow view of a portion of it.

By a narrow view, I mean a view that is unrelated to the whole life of mankind, past and future. Because it is not so related, it is misleading. Therefore, in each case, the workers are not helped to an understanding, but are misled.

"Economic history" turns out to be a mere record of the social changes in England (sometimes in Europe) from the Manorial system to the present day, without any attempt to show the forces that caused the change, and were the mainspring of events. These forces are reserved for a separate study, "economics" to wit, which either treats of an abstract "capitalism," with the minimum of historical reference, or, if it is the variety called "descriptive," describes the workings of bourgeois civilisation with the proud manner of a prison chaplain showing a Fabian around the cells.

In the case of "economic history," the last 1,000 years of England is so fascinating, even as a mere labelled collection of events and systems, that the workers—who are beginning to suspect "economic"—go on studying this history without any idea of how much more meaning and use could be found in it. They are exactly in the position of the naturalists of the 18th century. The mere survey of the varieties of animal and plant species was an interest in itself. But it was as nothing to the vision of life that was opened out to evolutionary biologists in the next century. In the same way there is the possibility of learning the past life of mankind in such a way as to understand how and *why* one kind of society grew out of another; and by this means to foresee the possible future of the workers and be moved to strive for it.

How is it, that in Britain this possibility has been withheld from the working-class? How is it that when an intelligent middle-class Socialist like Bernard Shaw wishes to take up his parable against Marxism, he is reduced to criticising, as the only available book, a contemptible production like Hyndman's "Evolution of Revolution." How is it that until Phillips Price's recent book on the class struggle in Germany there has never been a decent piece of historical or economic analysis written by an Englishman?

The answer is to be found without going into deeper causes, first, in the miserable mental poverty of the British bourgeois historians (on whom the Marxist reinterpreter must to a certain extent be dependent, unless he knows other languages), and secondly, in the character of those Marxian reinterpreters.

The calibre of the British university historian has been extraordinarily low. An exception occurs once in a century, like Gibbon or Maitland. But the ordinary don has been, in technical scholarship, far below the level of other European countries. His disability is due not to laziness or an inferior British brain—he can be as indefatigable and dry-as-dust as any—but to a profound lack of any conception that history is the study of mankind as a whole, or that the main factors in human history can be abstracted and analysed. Consequently, once our historians had ceased to accept the simple view of Macaulay, that history consisted in boosting the Whigs and the manufacturing bourgeoisie as the zenith of civilisation, they were utterly at a loss. Some of them, in despair, have even turned again to GOD under the impression that these three letters of the alphabet can somehow be linked up with the fruits of their historical researches. Some, like Acton, have taken comfort in the belief that some "principle" (variant of GOD) such as Liberty is at the bottom of it. But the majority have flatly abandoned any pretence of thinking at all. Mankind does not exist for them; only a particular set of problems in a particular epoch—juridicial, ecclesiastical, mensurational or what you will.

They know history, as a flea knows human anatomy.

Nowhere does their incapacity appear more than in their attitude to the Materialist Conception of History. Here is a unifying conception, about which there might be agreement or disagreement. Yet I have never met, I have never even heard of a modern professional historian who has taken the trouble to understand what this conception is. Instead, we hear an alarmed cackle, about "material and spiritual," or "economics doesn't explain everything," or "the driving force of idealism," or any other similar phase that will serve as a cloak for intelluctual sloth and cowardice.

Mr. Lloyd George's speech on "the wild and poisonous berries of Karl Marxism," may have been laughed at in the college Common Rooms, but it expressed their view, none the less. Perhaps some instinct warns these bourgeois historians, that, for their own sakes, Marx must not be understood. At any rate, their barbaric ignorance, alike of the meaning of history or the meaning of Marx, remains invincible. They are exactly like those African chiefs of the 'nineties who, not having the remotest conception of the enormous mechanism of a rapidly developing imperialism, held fast to the simple idea that everything was due to a Great White Queen.

But if the bourgeois historians are a sorry lot in Britain, the Marxists of the past 40 years have been also to blame. Of all the books that were written and circulated so widely between 1885 and 1905, there is not one than is widely read nowadays. Nor is there any reason to suppose that those more recently written will not meet the same fate. The reason is that I have already indicated. There has been going on this fractional distilling of Marxism, and with the happy result of being able to produce a variety of distillation products, to suit every purse and palate. But in the distillation there is broken up the whole spirit of Marxism, the unifying conception that could enable a struggling class to see and strike at the weak points in the defences of its enemy; and at the same time to realise its relation to the rest of mankind, and to know that in every conflict it fulfilled a historic mission.

It is, therefore, important for the workers in this country to have every opportunity of reading books wherein the significance of economic science and its wide scope are fully appreciated. This book by A. Bogdanoff, for instance, is called a Short Course of Economic Science; and "Economics," as it is usually understood, is only brought in as subsections in a survey which runs from primitive society, and feudal society, past the cul-de-sac of slave-owning society, and through serfdom up to merchant capitalism and present finance-capital. Human organisation begins with a struggle of man, in small groups, against the overmastering powers of nature. This is natural self-sufficing society. It is succeeded by commercial society, wherein the struggle of man is now against the overmastering strength of the social relations. This society is marked by the development of exchange, the growth of exchange fetishism, and internal class struggles. It is finally succeeded by socialist society, wherein, class struggles over, the struggle against

36

nature is resumed by mankind organised freely in a group, that covers the whole world. The synthesis is achieved. The prehistoric period of man comes to an end.

This has been the textbook of study groups in the Russian Communist Party since the late 'nineties. It is now translated for the first time. When a second edition is called for, or rather some considerable time before that event, the Party should make arrangements to have the book thoroughly edited, so that an index is added and, if possible a list of a few books of reference at the end of each chapter.

R.P.A.

The British Trades Union Congress at Bournemouth

NO doubt the members of the General Council are congratulating themselves on their lucky escape at Bournemouth. Less than a score of weeks after the General Strike and right in the midst of the miners' struggle it has been possible for a Trades Union Congress to be held without any discussion of the General Council's responsibilities.

Just before the Congress the "Times," the chief organ of the bourgeoisie, anxiously asked the question: "Will the General Strike prove to be the climax of militant trade unionism, or the beginning of a new phase culminating in definitely revolutionary aims?"

Therefore it is necessary to examine what happened at Bournemouth.

The main points are:

(1) The General Council successfully burked any discussion of the General Strike or of its responsibility therein.

(2) The General Council successfully substituted a bureaucratic conference to be called at a date chosen by themselves, for the Trades Union Congress.

(3) The General Council secured the agreement of the miners' leaders to these two decisions.

(4) The increase of the power of the General Council was rejected.

(5) The letter from the All-Russian Council of Trade Unions and its reception.

39

(6) The chairman's references to International Trade Union Unity.

(7) Purcell's attitude to International Trade Union Unity.

(8) The General Council's attack on the Minority Movement.

(9) The new and still more Right-wing policy put forward for the trade unions (Pugh's speech).

On the first and second points it should be understood that the General Council is elected by the Trades Union Congress and is wholly responsible thereto. It is true that in July, 1925, and also in April, 1926, the General Council summoned a special conference composed of the Executive Committees of the unions affiliated to the Trades Union Congress. But this does not by any means absolve the General Council from its duty of making a full report to the Trades Union Congress.

Such a report was not made, and the General Council escaped without any censure for devoting only a brief paragraph to the General Strike. Thus, the trade union leaders did not only escape the discussion of their responsibility; they also managed to substitute, as the highest authority in the trade union movement, the bureaucratically composed Conference of Executives for the more representative Trades Union Congress. They were also able to secure the agreement of the miners both to the burking of discussion and to the establishment of a sort of House of Lords in the form of a Conference of officials. It was an error on the part of the miners' leaders, due to a mistaken belief that the unity of the movement could be secured by covering up real differences and hiding crimes committed against the working class.

This opportunist belief in formal unity (which contains within itself a real disbelief in the powers of the working class itself) had the gravest possible consequences. The working class was told that the General Council refused to allow itself to be put on trial—and then was informed that the Miners' Federation had connived at this policy!

Again, it was fully in conformity with this policy that the Right-wing leaders of the trade unions refused to increase the powers of the General Council. To have increased the powers of the General Council would have meant that formally and constitutionally the British Trades Union Congress would have possessed the powers which now belong only to the bureaucratic Conference of Executives. This would have robbed the bureaucrats of their retreat.

The refusal of more power to the General Council was a concrete expression of the defeatist attitude which had already been revealed by the General Strike. In point of fact this defeatist attitude had existed from Scarborough onwards. The Scarborough Trades Union Congress showed a ready disposition to pass resolutions of a militant nature, but showed also a great disinclination to pass resolutions, or even to deal with questions, that necessitated immediate action. The more urgent and practical the question, the less was it discussed at the Scarborough Congress.

At Scarborough a resolution to give more power was rejected and a resolution was carried which instructed the Council to examine the problem in all its bearings, with power to consult the Executives of affiliated unions, and to report to a special conference of the Executives concerned their considered recommendations on the subject. That special conference was never called. Now, a year later, a similar proposal moved by one of the more militant unions was rejected by a majority.

The ultra-reactionary secretary of the railwaymen, Mr. Cramp, said that the N.U.R. was opposed to any extension of the powers of the General Council because it could not be made effective. This is the same Mr. Cramp who signed a humiliating agreement on behalf of the railwaymen declaring the strike to have been wrong and humbly promising not to repeat the offence. Considerations of loyalty (to the bosses) clearly forbade him to agree to any further increase in the powers of the General Council. Thus whilst at Scarborough the resolutions on the organisational question only indicated the preservation of the reactionary character of the so-called trade union leaders under the cloak of radical phraseology at Bournemouth the defeat of the resolution proposed by the Minority Movement unmasked once and for all the "Left" trade union strike-breakers (such as Purcell, Pugh and others).

Still another Scarborough resolution throws light upon Bournemouth. At Scarborough the Congress instructed the General Council to do everything in their power to secure world-wide unity of the trade union movement. This resolution was interpreted by the new General Council, to *mean* "everything in their power," a very small quantity! After the Amsterdam International meeting at the beginning of December, 1925, had turned down the unity proposals, it had been agreed by the Anglo-Russian Committee to go ahead with the calling of a world conference. But the majority of the General Council turned this proposal down, and Amsterdam had the best of it.

For some months the General Council was able to maintain the rôle of Mr. Facing-Both-Ways on this question. Then came the General Strike, when the splendid help offered by the Soviet trade unionists to the British workers transformed what seemed unreal to the trade union leaders into something very real to the working class of Britain and of the whole world. International Trade Union Unity had been translated into terms of fact for every miner, and for wide circles of the proletariat. In the eyes of the toiling masses the Anglo-Russian Committee was no longer simply a leaders' alliance, but had become the organisational expression of a direct alliance between the proletariat of Great Britain and that of the Soviet Union.

In the light of these considerations it can be understood why the General Council, after prolonged hesitation, were prepared to meet again in the Anglo-Russian Committee, but considered the Committee and its decisions of no importance and deemed it necessary to keep them secret. This also explains why the leaders of the General Council were compelled to bring forward once more the Scarborough resolution affirming the need for international trade union unity and also why they had to agree to the proposal of the Soviet trade unionists that a world conference should be summoned *within two months* of the date of the Trades Union Congress at Bournemouth.

When the letter from the All-Russian Council of Trade Unions arrived, in place of the fraternal delegation, forbidden by the British Government, and this letter was found to contain fraternal greetings and serious criticism, the General Council could do nothing but misbehave itself. They had nothing to say, so they reprinted the letter in its abbreviated telegraphese so as to make it look grotesque. They circulated this to the delegates, with an angry protest couched in solemn and pompous phraseology. The bourgeois press naturally hailed the General's Council's outburst as a "calm and dignified protest."

At Bournemouth two speakers dealt with the subject of unity. The first was the chairman, Arthur Pugh, the second was A. A. Purcell, who, besides being one of the prominent members of the General Council, holds the position of chairman of the Amsterdam International. These speeches were not exactly the same in outlook, but past experience seems to show that inside the General Council there will be no difficulty in harmonising, or at any rate, concealing differences over so long a period as to have the same effect as harmony.

Pugh said:

"We run the risk of laying too much stress upon a merely formal and mechanical unity in the field of the international trade union movement. A mere fusion of existing trade union bodies would fail to bring real unity.

43

Unless there be a common will and purpose there cannot be a common conception of aims and methods, and of the ends to be served by international co-operation."

What does this mean? It is not difficult to guess.

Pugh's views do not differ very much from those of Oudegeest and Sassenbach. This alliance was also confirmed in Purcell's speech. "How are the difficulties standing in the way of International unity to be over come?" asks this renegade. "It is for the Russians to ease the situation." From Purcell's lips this means "a little less Bolshevism please"!

The friction in connection with the subject of unity has shown that even in respect to this main "commanding post" of the bankrupt "Left," position after position has been handed over to Thomas and MacDonald. Purcell, Pugh and Co., have completed their full "left wheel" and come back to the starting point, finding themselves face to face with Oudegeest.

Lastly, the chairman's speech set forth the new policy of the new Right-wing of the trade unions. Pugh, dealing with wages policy said: "Has not the time arrived to consider how they could apply the principle of wages guaranteeing a corresponding index of national production?" This of course is simply tying the workers' standard of life to what the industry can afford; in other words, as the process of the decline of capitalist production becomes more acute, the position of the workers is to become gradually worse.

This is then all that reformism has to offer as a policy for the workers. A "scientific" depression of the standard of life, it contrasts in a significant way with the statement made by Pugh earlier in his address. "It had been the historic task of trade unionism to raise the standard of working class life."

The above summary of the outstanding features of the Trades Union Congress are nearly all of them apparent victories for the Right-wing. But to conclude from this that the

Bournemouth Congress was in every respect a failure or a backward step would be a mistake. In the first place it is clear that in this Congress there was a very high temperature existing below the surface coolness. This fact is very explicitly pointed out by Ellen Wilkinson, in her article in "Lansbury's Weekly," where she says that 97 per cent. of the delegates were thinking of nothing but the General Strike.

Two facts attest this real position: first there is the incident when the Congress had to be adjourned for at hour because of a complete hold up of the business. The Miners' Federation objected to the choice of Mr. Bromley (who had done his best to break the strike) as the supporter of the resolution pledging the aid of the Congress to the miners. Headed by McGurk, a representative from Lancashire, one of the poorest mining areas, they refused to hear Bromley and sang the "Red Flag" until the meeting was closed down.

We have the further significant fact that on all important questions there was a steady minority of not less than 700,000. This 700,000 does not include the miners.

In the second place, even if we had not these very significant facts, Bournemouth still would not be a failure. To register the Congress as a Right-wing success, as a step backward in the class struggle, would be to misconceive the whole position, would be to forget that there had been a General Strike.

Far from judging the General Strike in the light of Bournemouth, Bournemouth must be judged in the light of the General Strike. The significance of the General Strike cannot be over-estimated insofar as its immediate effects are concerned. But whether its effects mature rapidly or slowly it constitutes the biggest departure in the history of the British working class since Chartist times. Therefore all forces and organisations must be viewed in relation to the strike. In the short space of this article it is possible only to select three things: the General Council, the new Left-wing that is arising, and the Communist

45

Party.

It is now clear that the General Council being nominally elected by Congress and really appointed by the respective trade unions may not represent accurately the will of the Congress, even though it may manœuvre the Congress into subsequent acceptance of what it has done. Secondly, the Congress itself is only to a limited extent representative of the rank and file, and must have its standing orders and its constitution revised before it can be truly representative.

There now exists an alliance between Thomas and Purcell, none the less definite in that they are probably not fully conscious of it themselves. It is not intentions, but actions that matter. The General Strike was like an earthquake removing landmarks. Purcell may still measure the inches that separate him from Thomas, but their common signature to the General Council's report (published by what the "Times" called Mr. Bromley's "calculated indiscretion") removes them both miles away from the workers' struggle. However, the most important thing is the fact that the Congress has shown what a stride forward the *process of political growth* has made in the British Labour movement. The powerful growth—coming from below —of the new genuine Left-wing, which has already brought under its influence a million and a quarter British proletarians, has found its expression in energetic opposition to the General Council.

The leaders of the new Left, unknown figures emerging from the real movement of the workers, appeared for the first time on the scene during the General Strike, then in the Miners' Federation conference (where a majority showed itself more Left than Cook, rejecting the Bishops' Memorandum). They became more noticeable in the miners' activities during their prolonged struggle (the miners and the miners' wives are learning more politics this summer than they have done for thirty years and more); at the Minority Movement conferences (which expressed their growth, size, significance and tempo); in the real sympathy and solidarity everywhere shown to the Soviet workers (the five million rouble gift electrified the British working class and made them think); and finally in the influx of workers into the Communist Party.

It is of the utmost importance that this new Left should grow up as rapidly as possible, should not be allowed to stray into barren activities and policies, but should from the beginning come under the ideological influence and practical guidance of the Party, which should do its utmost towards the organisational coordination of the opposition.

The Communist Party

But after the General Strike vacillations *to the Right* in the ranks of the British Communist Party, or rather in its leadership, became observable, which demand the most determined rectification.

The basis of these vacillations is an inadequate comprehension of all the tremendous profundity of the moves that have taken place inside the British proletariat. This lack of understanding was first of all displayed in a number of errors connected with the *Anglo-Russian Committee*. Whereas the viewpoint of the opposition in the Soviet C.P. demanding the *rupture* of the Anglo-Russian Committee is profoundly erroneous, so on the other hand the refusal to criticise sharply the treacherous conduct of the General Council leaders is also a grave error. Such a position, shielding "generous" endeavours to preserve the Anglo-Russian Committee at any cost, objectively means aid to the opportunists.

This tendency has several times displayed itself in the ranks of the British Communist Party. The British Communist Party has spoken a language much less clear than the Russian trade unions; the British Communist Party in particular adopted a mild attitude towards the "Lefts" of the Purcell type, although these "Left" leaders had moved to the *Right*, to an alliance with

Thomas. The British Communist Party has practically not criticised Cook at all, although Cook has succeeded in making a large number of errors.

The erroneous policy of the Communist Party was particularly clearly shown at the conference of the Minority Movement and then at the Trades Union Congress at Bournemouth, not to mention the demand for the recalling of the parliamentary Labour Party from the House of Commons. This was a great error. For in order to denounce these opportunists who are so loyal to the Government, it is not a demand for withdrawal from Parliament, incomprehensible to the masses, that is necessary, but demands for defending the fighting miners, for merciless denunciation of the Government's position, etc. A much bigger error, fraught with possible grave consequences, was the decision made at the Executive Committee of the Minority Movement to restrict themselves to a mild criticism of the *General Council*. Instead of concentrating during the Congress all the force of their blows on the treacherous position of the General Council, a decision was passed having *just the opposite significance*. By this the M.M. unconsciously aided the General Council to blur over the question of responsibility for the defeat of the General Strike.

At the T.U.C. the miners' leader, A. J. Cook, vacillated sharply towards the General Council, voting against a discussion on the General Strike. The Left opposition opposed Cook. This shows the entire depths of the move *to the Left* amongst the working masses. After Cook had done this, he admitted his mistake, but he did not think over all its profundity to the very end.

Only superficial observers can write as the "Workers' Weekly" did on September 10th, that "as compared with Scarborough, Bournemouth is a step back." It is a "step back" only insofar as the "Left" bureaucracy, such as Purcell and Co., are drifting back. In reality Bournemouth has shown what a tremendous step forward has been made by the *working masses*.

48

A few months back Cook was the "most Left of all." And now more than a million votes at the Congress prove to be *much more to the Left than Cook.* This should be thoroughly understood. And if it is thoroughly understood, the necessary conclusions must be drawn: vacillations to the Right must be abandoned, and all energy must be devoted to a denunciation of the traitors and capitulators still sitting on the backs of the British proletariat.

We consider it necessary to state the errors of the British Communist Party openly in the firm hope that they will rapidly and easily be corrected. The British Communist Party has a tremendous future and the fewer mistakes it makes (which are particularly harmful now in the critical phase of the movement) the more quickly will it become the great mass Party of the British workers.

The Russian Revolution

THIS month of November, ten years ago, was the Bolshevik revolution; this month of November, 1927, there still is the Bolshevik revolution, the same, but grown greater. The challenge that rang out in November, 1917, has swollen in volume through the years, and has filled the whole earth till now in every land the capitalists cannot get the sound of it out of their ears. To none is the challenge more compelling than to the leaders of the trade unions and the co-operative societies and the political labour organisations. Their answer is—to deny that any challenge exists. This is the meaning of the flood of anniversary articles in which the revolution is treated as some huge unique catastrophe, as something peculiar to Russia, something that *has* happened.

This treatment of the revolution, isolating it, gaping at it, is akin to the canonisation of revolutionary leaders (like the turning of Marx into a hackneyed Liberal). Those who would understand the revolution must seek to understand the process of human history. In that search they will find not only that within the historic period man advances by means of class struggle, but that within the period of capitalism class struggle after class struggle culminates in revolution. Within the last hundred and fifty years alone history presents itself not as a record of kings and battles, but (in spite of all the systematic lying of the Whigs and the Radicals, set forth in every school book, in every scholarly tome, in every speech, sermon and editorial) as a process of class striving with class, culminating in the overthrow of one class another, the intervening periods being but the preparation for that overthrow.

The American Revolution reacts on the great French Revolution from which in turn there issue the revolutions of 1930 and 1848 (in England the Luddites of 1812, and the suppressed trade union agitation oft 1800 to 1825, are

51

succeeded by the Chartist movement of the working class which in its widest sense spans the years from the late 'twenties to the early 'fifties). Already in 1848 the working class has learned that it must go forward in its own strength; and though the Paris Commune, the firms attempt to destroy capitalist rule and to build a workers' society is drowned in blood, the lessons of these few weeks remain unforgotten throughout the epoch of imperialism that followed. Then as the violence, punitive expeditions, wars, and massacres of imperialism bring more and more colonial peoples beneath the yoke, the stage is reached of dividing up the spoil anew through the first imperialist world war; and when this stage is reached the decay of imperialism becomes manifest, and equally manifest the rising of new forces, the re-awakening of the working class, the first rally of the colonial peoples against oppression. The revolution of 1905 in Russia marks the beginning of the decline, 1917 the end of the rotten rule of imperialism over one-sixth part of the earth; and at the same time an intenser conflict begins against capitalist oppression in every country. In the midst of this intenser conflict the British working class now finds itself compelled to fight for a livelihood, and in that struggle to attack the whole system that refuses it the bread of life. This the process of world history, this is the meaning of the stage in that process in which we live, this is the meaning of the Russian Revolution.

How do they see it, the leaders of Labour, the bureaucracy of the trade unions and the co-operative societies, the men elected to parliaments and municipalities? In what shape do they perceive the Russian Revolution? The answer, as shown by thousands of their speeches and articles, is that for them it is something remote, spectacular, inexplicable, and, at close quarters, dangerous. And beneath this surface gaping there lurks a real hostility, only partially restrained by philistine respectfulness towards the might of the Soviet State.

The hostility bursts forth again and again, both in decisions of policy, from the Democracy and Socialism thesis of the Bern International in 1919 up to the rupture of the Anglo-Russian Committee as a pendant to the Baldwin Government's rupture of the Trade Agreement, and also in the declamations of leading "Socialists." It is especially at the moments when the Soviet power appears least strong that their theoretical objections become most pronounced. "The Bolsheviks," wrote Brailsford, ten years ago, against the first activity of the revolution to bring peace, "are putting themselves outside the pale of our international Socialist society." And through all the vicissitudes that make up a Brailsford, he is in the end as he was in the beginning, impenitently opposed to the world revolution. And Brailsford is typical of all the "Socialists" that pretend to welcome the revolution.

How is this attitude to be explained? It is the outlook born of the between-times, born of the trough of time that lies between the wave-crests of the advancing revolution.

In this century such an attitude was common amongst the Menshevik Socialists in Russia after the 1905 revolution. Because revolution had been defeated once, therefore revolution was at all times and for ever impossible. The Labour Movement, they said, must work within the framework of Tsardom, and give up the dream of its overthrow. So, to their eternal shame and dishonour, these "Socialists" argued—until 1917 swept them into oblivion along with the rotten timbers to which they clung. So now in this country, in the trough of the wave, in a similar time of depression, instead of fighting, stimulating, and heartening the workers, they are preaching industrial peace (submission to the worst the employers can inflict), and dropping Socialism out of their programme. The Edinburgh Trades Union Congress and the Blackpool Conference of the Labour Party mark the lowest pitch of fatalism, of craven submission to circumstance, of complete failure of courage and hope on the part of the leaders.

But this outlook is inevitable amongst men thus blind to the real meaning of the working-class struggle and to the movement it imparts to history. How shall savages understand an eclipse of the sun? To savages, knowing naught of the planetary laws of motion, or the periods of the moon, the sun's eclipse is a catastrophe without past or future, unpredictable, causeless, dire, and destructive. To the astronomer the eclipse, itself predictable, is the means to verify and establish even more fundamental laws of physics. So with the Russian Revolution. Those who swallowed the hocus-pocus of capitalist politics and disdained any knowledge that lay beyond their own noses, were at once astonished by the revolution (an accident they had not allowed for—like the war which was also left out of their reckonings) and have never ceased to be wrong about it since; and because they were wrong about it, because their scheme of the human universe never rose above the conception of living from hand to mouth, they were bound to mislead the workers in their every-day struggle.

Further, the analogy, if followed up, yields a still more startling parallel between the astronomer of the skies and the social astronomer thinking in the discipline of Marxism. The most learned savage of an Oxford common room, the most bedizened medicine-man on the Treasury Bench, or at the Guildhall Banquet, is less capable of understanding social phenomena than the simple "ignorant" working man who can tell a capitalist war when he sees it (when the savages are prating of nationality, justice, &c.. &c.), and who can see that mankind will halt and retreat unless the capitalists are thrown from off the backs of the workers.

Social astronomers, able to calculate the laws of motion of capitalist society, predict the world revolution; and (since man himself is a social force) strive to hasten it. In the Union of Socialist Soviet Republics the endeavour is to build a Socialist society; and in capitalist Britain to build up through daily struggles a workers' movement that will conquer the power the governing class, and along with the revolutionary classes of India and other lands, set free a quarter of the human race.

The Meerut Sentences

The Meerut prisoners have been sentenced. After nearly four years in the stifling jail of Meerut, held without bail and tried without jury, they receive sentences of transportation for life, for twelve years, for ten years.

What Devil's Island meant in the calendar of French Imperialism, what northern-most Siberia meant in the record of the Tsardom, that transportation has meant in the annals of British India. The penal settlements, and of these the Andaman Islands are the most used and the best known, are a bye-word for the horrors inflicted on their inmates, fever-ridden swamps, where disease and death commute the government sentences of long-term imprisonment.

These men had dared to help in the organisation of trade unions, they had dared to lead mass strikes and to develop the class character of the workers' struggle in India. Through their efforts and through the lessons of the strike they led, the Indian workers were rapidly overcoming the weaknesses of the earlier period and as a consequence were growing increasingly conscious of themselves as a class, and had taken the first steps to independent struggle and leadership of the whole struggle of the Indian masses.

For this the vengeance of imperialism falls upon them in this series of savage sentences:

Muzaffar Ahmad, Vice-President of the All-India Trade Union Congress, already sentenced to four years' imprisonment in the Cawnpore conspiracy trial of 1924, is sentenced to transportation for life.

Philip Sprat, executive member of the All-India Trade Union Congress, active in trade union work and in the co-operative movement when in England, is

55

sentenced to transportation for twelve years.

S.V. Ghate, Vice-President of the Bombay Municipal Workers' Union, and in 1927 appointed Assistant Secretary of the All-India Trade Union Congress—transportation for twelve years.

K.N. Joglekar, organising secretary, G.I.P. Railwaymen's Union—transportation for twelve years.

R.S. Nimbkar, President Bombay Oil Co.'s Employees Union, Secretary Bombay Trades Council—transportation for twelve years.

S.A. Dange, General Secretary of the Girni Kamgar Union (which lead the six months' Bombay cotton strike of 1928), and Assistant Secretary of the All-India Trade Union Congress—transportation for twelve years.

B.F. Bradley, formerly of the London District Committee of the Amalgamated Engineering Union, member of the Executive Council of the Girni Kamgar Union, and Treasurer of the joint strike committee during the Bombay cotton strike—transportation for ten years.

S.S. Mirajkar, Secretary of the British India Steam Navigation Co. Staff Union—transportation for ten years.

S. Usmani, delegate to the All-India Trade Union Congress, previously sentenced in the 1924 Cawnpore trial—transportation for ten years.

P.C. Joshi, Editor of Kranti Kari and Secretary of United Provinces Workers' and Peasants' Party—transportation for seven years.

D. Goswami, Organiser of the Bengal Jute Workers' Union—seven years' transportation.

Abdul Majid, left India to fight for the Khilafat in 1920, and visited Russia—seven years' transportation.

G.M. Adhikari, a doctor of engineering, M.G. Desai, an Indian journalist; S.S. Josh, president of the first All-India Workers and Peasants' Party in December, 1928; A. Prasad, all prominent workers in the Indian Labour Movement—transportation for five years.

Those who received four years' rigorous imprisonment were: G. Chakravarty, leader of the Kharagpur Railway strike, official of the East India Railway Union; R.R. Mitra, General Secretary of the Bengal Jute Workers' Union; Gopal Basak, official of the Bengal Textile Union; Lester Hutchinson, Editor of the New Spark, after the arrest of the others elected to an official position in the Girni Kamgar Union; S.H. Jhabwalla, General Secretary of the G.I.P. Railwaymen's Union (with 41,000 members); K.N. Sehgal, member of the All-India Congress Committee.

Those sentenced to three years rigorous imprisonment were: S. Huda, Secretary of the Transport Workers Union of Bengal; A.A. Alwe, President of the Girni Kamgar Union; R. Kasle, official of the Girni Kamgar Union; Gourakshanker, member of the Workers and Peasants Party; L.R. Khadam, prominent worker in the Labour Movement.

Three were acquitted, while in the case of another, D.R. Thengdi, pioneer of the Indian Trade Union Movement and a veteran Nationalist, British imperialism was cheated of its victim by the old man's death in prison.

When the news of these dreadful sentences was received in Bombay, the Girni Kamgar Union called a strike in protest. It was a sign that the cotton workers of Bombay, who get neither insurance benefit nor P.A.C. relief, for whom to strike means to face starvation, understood very well that the right of trade union organisation is at stake.

The issue is nothing less than this, as indeed is indicated by the list of who the prisoners are, whether the capitalists are to be allowed to root out trade unionism in India.

This is not how the prosecution put it. They charged the prisoners, in the portentous language of the Indian Penal Code, that they conspired to deprive the King-Emperor of the Sovereignty of British India.

This was accompanied by a long rigmarole about the Communist International, which blossomed out in the speech of the prosecuting counsel into the statement that the object of the accused "was, in effect, to substitute for the Government of His Majesty, the Government of Mr. Stalin, as he is now called."

But in the whole three years and ten months of the trial, from arrest to sentence, not a single overt act, which could deprive the King-Emperor of his Sovereignty, could be proved against them. Their "offence" was to have stimulated, encouraged and led the fight against the terrible oppressions and poverty imposed by British Imperialism upon the toiling masses of India. This is "conspiracy against the King."

On the other hand, for the 1928 cotton strike alone the prosecution produced *seven hundred* of the usual garbled police reports of speeches, to prove the "incitement of antagonism between Capital and Labour."

That is to say, the prisoners were sentenced for doing just what every fighting trade unionist in this country is found doing during a strike, and for saying just what is daily said in our trade union branches. The Meerut trial therefore is in the first place an attack on the workers' right of trade union organisation. The sentences strike at the root of trade unionism. The international working class, and above all, the British working class, is bound to fight against these sentences and not

58

to cease the struggle until the sentences have been cancelled and the prisoners released.

Trade unionism in India in the real sense begins with the Meerut prisoners. The name, trade union, had not existed before 1918, and the meagre trade unions that grew up after that date, were vessels without contents; not trade union organisations, but trade union offices, in which sat middle-class philanthropists and lawyers, generals without an army and without an enemy. In a word, this trade union movement in name only, tolerated by the government as harmless and even useful, became the prey of every sort of adventurer and opportunist who used it as a jumping-off ground for a seat in the legislative assembly or a post under the government.

The Meerut prisoners brought life and fight into these unions, increased their membership and organised the trade union movement in trades hitherto unorganised. The great strikes at the end of the war had thrown up forms of trade union organisation which were little more than strike committees and these had vanished like the transient organisations of the early strike movement in Great Britain.

The Meerut trial and sentences represent therefore the attempt of British Imperialism to strangle at birth a great historical working-class movement, in a country whose population comprises one-sixth of mankind.

British imperialism has its reasons for this. Indian trade unions have to protect workers against the most miserable conditions, of wages (1d an hour), hours (limited in 1922 to a 60-hour week), and general working conditions. If Marx could tell how the millocracy of England used up three. generations of cotton operatives in one lifetime, an even worse tale must be told in India during the "beneficent" rule of the sahibs, when the expectation of life has fallen within a generation from 30 to 22, or less than half the average expectation of life in England.

The fight of an organised Indian working class against

such conditions as these would threaten the very basis of Imperialism, the super-profits on which the British capitalists fatten.

The Indian working class could not be bribed as were sections of the English working class in the later nineteenth century by crumbs from the rich man's banquet of super profits, for they themselves are the source of super-profits. The Indian trade unions, if real, as the Meerut prisoners were making them, were bound to be of the same sort as the Chartist trade unions, and could never sink into the torpor and friendly society condition of the British craft unions in the latter part of the nineteenth century.

But the parallel with Chartism is insufficient. The Indian trade union movement is being born in the epoch of Imperialism, amid wars and revolutions, in the country that is a blazing furnace of colonial revolt against Imperialism.

Born in these circumstances, the Indian trade unions are bound to be but a first step. The Indian proletariat once aware of itself as a class, enters on a road when of necessity it is bound to organise trade unions, to organise its own independent working class party, to take the lead of the peasantry, to lead the whole national struggle for emancipation, and to find its goal (though not its final goal) in the overthrow of Imperialism, the independence of India, and the complete destruction of the feudal-imperialist regime.

British Imperialism recognises its deadliest enemy in the Indian working class and for this reason, tries to crush its advance by a reign of terror and sentences of transportation.

For this reason, too, because there is no reconciling of the interests of the Indian workers with the interests of the Imperialist bourgeoisie, all other interests and all parties are bound to take up their positions on one side or other. The British Labour Party, and the Trade Union Congress General Council, abandon their humanitarian pose when colonial super-profits are at stake (for they share in these super-profits) and condemn the Meerut prisoners, only blaming the Government for not finishing them off more quickly. A sentiment with which the Tory Secretary of State for India cordially agreed, "this trial has gone on far too long," as he said when he took over this hangman's job from the Labour Government.

The pharisees of the General Council, celebrating this year the centenary of the Dorchester Labourers (sentenced to seven years' transportation a hundred years ago for organising trade unions in England), would not raise a finger to release the men who were organising trade unions in India.

On the other hand, the organisation of the Indian capitalists, the Indian National Congress, when faced by the sharpening class struggle, abandons its opposition to the "Satanic" British Raj, and its representative, Gandhi, signed a pact with the Viceroy which released 50,000 political captives, but kept the Meerut prisoners fast in their gaol.

The Meerut prisoners' trial and sentences raise the whole question of the right of workers to organise trade unions in a colonial country, where the masses are held down by naked force. For British Imperialism it is too dangerous, and for Gandhi and Lansbury also. But for British workers it is an elementary duty, which they cannot fail to carry through, to support the fight of working-class organisation in India, and to join with the Indian workers in their struggle against British Imperialism.

It is not only a duty: it is a necessity. Not only is it true that a nation that oppresses another cannot itself be free; but the same Imperialist class that is oppressing India, is oppressing and robbing the workers of this country by wage-cuts and speed-up, tariffs and taxes, is taking the bread out of the mouths of the workers' children, depriving them of the benefits of education, insurance and all other social services, and casting into gaol Tom Mann or any other leader of working class revolt. The railwaymen facing a wage-cut, the busmen on strike against

61

speed-up, the Lancashire workers suffering under the Midland Agreement, are fighting the same class that would deny the Indian workers the right to organise.

But the deepest significance of the Meerut Trial and the reason for the extreme ferocity of the sentences, is that the representatives of the Indian masses and the representatives of the British working class were carrying on a united struggle against British Imperialism. For a hundred and fifty years British Capitalism has been a parasite on India, sucking its life-blood. For a hundred and fifty years every device of imperialist propaganda has been used to sunder the exploited of India from the exploited of Britain.

It is the glory of the Meerut prisoners that for the first time on such a charge representatives of the exploited classes of India and Britain stood together. Their stand is a symbol of that unity of the British working class with the masses of the British Empire which alone can destroy British Imperialism. For a hundred and fifty years British Capitalism has been a parasite on India, sucking its life-blood. For a hundred and fifty years every device of imperialist propaganda has been used to sunder the exploited of India from the exploited of Britain.

The Meerut prisoners, Englishmen and Indians in the dock together, destroyed once and for all the jingo picture of "black men" versus "white men," of "Asiatics against Europeans" and showed the true line of cleavage in a fight of the oppressed of both nations against the oppressors. To obtain their release, therefore, must be the object of both British and Indian workers. But it is the British Governments—Tory, Labour and National—that have kept them in prison. It is the British Government which is responsible for the sentence. The biggest responsibility lies with the British working class to secure their release, by nation-wide agitation in every organisation, in every kind of meeting.

The feeling of horror and indignation that was felt in the middle of January when the sentences were announced must grow into a powerful agitation that will force open the prison doors, annul these venomous sentences, and establish the workers' right to organisation in India.

William Morris Versus the Morris Myth

WILLIAM MORRIS is a name in the working-class movement of Britain. His revolutionary poems, almost our only native revolutionary poems, are sung at May Day demonstrations. His memory is revered by those who can recall him, especially his plain, simple habit of speech, essence of straightforwardness and revolutionary vigor. His revolutionary Socialist writings still have an influence, and would have more, but for the veil with which the capitalists have surrounded him. For, more than almost any other socialist leader of the 19th century, Morris has been subjected to that "canonisation" of which Lenin spoke.

This month the centenary of Morris's birth is being celebrated, and the final sanctification of him as a "harmless saint" is being carried through. Consequently, the first task is to clear away the nuisance that the capitalists are committing on the name of Morris before any estimate of him can be attempted.

There are several myths about William Morris, of which the most important are the bourgeois on the one hand, and the Labour Party and I.L.P. myth on the other. Already the bourgeois myth is proclaimed with the choice of Mr. Baldwin to open the William Morris Exhibition at the Victoria and Albert Museum last month. In Mr. Baldwin's speech, and in the newspaper comments upon it, there is no mention whatever of as a revolutionary. He is a great poet, a great craftsman, a great artist, a great influence, a great what-not; but he is not mentioned as a revolutionary. The capitalists were not always as impudent as this. When Mr. Asquith delivered his Romanes Lectures at Oxford on the Great Victorians, he significantly omitted William Morris from the list. But now the Tory leader of the House of Commons — representative of the capitalist class, of "these foul swine" as they are called in *The Dream of John Ball* — has the impudence to scatter his dirt over the memory of the man who said, of Parliament, that it was

> on the one side a kind of watch committee, sitting to see that the interests of the upper classes took no hurt, and on the other hand a sort of blind to delude the people into supposing that they had some share in the management of their own affairs.

Of course Morris was a great artist and a great craftsman; but neither his art nor his craftsman's work can be truly understood, nor can the whole man be understood, unless he is seen as he really was, as a revolutionary Socialist, fighting for the overthrow of capitalism and for the victory of the working class; and neither the capitalist politicians, nor the tribe of official biographers will be able to rob the working class of his memory and his teachings.

The Labour Party and I.L.P. myth is of a different character. It pictures Morris as a gentle Socialist, and fits in well with what Mr. Ramsay MacDonald, as leader of the I.L.P., once said of Socialism — his Socialism, the I.L.P. Socialism — as being based not upon economics, but as having a historical, ethical "and literary" basis. William Morris was hardly dead before this myth began to be built up by Bruce Glasier and many others, until at the present day it is being spread by literary ghouls like J. Middleton Murry — whose prolonged sessions on the grave of Morris, however, will neither give him the life blood of Morris nor distort the memory of what Morris was. The main burden of this myth, as it has lasted for over thirty years, is that Morris was "not a Marxist", and if there is now some assimilation of Morris and Marx in their scribblings, it is only because they have at length created a mythical Marx to fit in with their mythical Morris. It does not matter to them that his first political writings display his consciousness of class antagonism and class hatred; that these writings, beginning with the influence of what are called Ruskin's Socialist teachings, became more and more filled with the influence of Marx; that he joined a Marxist organisation; that, like Marx and Engels, he distrusted and fought the adventurer Hyndman, that along with Marx's daughter, Eleanor, and other close associates, he founded a second Marxist organisation: that he attended the Marxist International Congress in Paris in 1889, while Hyndman ranged himself with the opposition (possibilist) Congress: and that in his whole writings during the period of his political activity, Morris is accepting and following as best he can the teachings of Marx on economics, the class struggle and the victory of the working class through a period of civil war.

It should be realised that there is no question at all of these people weighing up the mistakes of Morris, as Engels did, estimating his grievous errors in tactics and concluding that he was all the less a Marxist for these things. No. They simply brush aside the Morris that was and construct a Morris that never existed, a sort of sickly dilettante socialist, as personally incredible as he would be politically monstrous.

What was the cause of this myth-building? The early myth-mongers of the I.L.P., all of them bitterly anti-Marxist, found it intolerable that an artist whom some of them regarded as a new Michaelangelo or new Leonardo da Vinci should be counted a follower of Marx. So that in essence the fight over the body of Morris was a fight against the influence of Marx inside the Labour movement; and unfortunately the only Socialist society on a class-struggle basis was dominated by H.M. Hyndman, whose bitter antagonism to made him ready to hand over Morris's memory to the I.L.P. traducers without a struggle.

The result is to this day even old associates of Morris will calmly state that he had not even studied Marx. What evidence is brought forward for this? Can it be believed that the only substantial evidence is his statement (since repeated over and over in books about him) that:

> Whereas I thoroughly enjoyed the historical part
> of *Capital*, I suffered agonies of confusion of the brain

over reading the pure economics of that great work.

Everyone knows that the first chapters of *Capital* are difficult; as much is stated by Marx himself as well as by Engels (and also by Lenin), and the only meaning of this sentence is that Morris was honest enough to confess his difficulties. Yet, actually, the meaning of this sentence was somehow twisted to make the proof that Morris was an anti-Marxist. Starting from the axiom "Morris an anti-Marxist", they then proceed on the evidence of ill-remembered gossip to rule out all in his writings that is evidence to the contrary.

It will be valuable to take two examples. J. Bruce Glasier in his book on Morris (published in 1921), shamelessly tries to show that the historical sketch, known as *Socialism, its Growth and Outcome*, by William Morris and Belfort Bax, does not represent the true views of Morris, though even his shamelessness might have been put to flight by the last sentence of the preface, signed by Morris and Bax, and reading as follows:

> We have only further to add that the work has been in the true sense of the word a *collaboration*, each sentence having been carefully considered by both the authors in common, although now one, now the other, has had more to do with initial suggestions in different portions of the work.

But it was clear that the chapters of that book, dealing with scientific socialism and Karl Marx, with their anti-Fabian and anti-I.L.P. outlook, had to be discounted at all costs.

But the virulence of the myth appears most strongly in relation to Morris's best-known book, *News from Nowhere.*

In this case the poison ivy of the myth has completely

hidden the oak. Almost everyone appears to have read *News from Nowhere* under the domination of the I.L.P. myth and have, consequently, read not what was in the book but what they expected to find.

Whereas the essence of "News from Nowhere" is *the insistence on the necessity of an armed rising and bitter civil war as the only path to socialism for the working class.*

Thirty years later it took all the force of Lenin's genius and profound knowledge of Marxism to restore in a revolutionary epoch the actual teachings of Marx and Engels. So much the easier was it for the myth-mongers to smother up the teachings of Marx forty-five years ago.

News from Nowhere was written at a time when the vapid counterrevolutionary book of Bellamy, *Looking Backwards*, had just been published and when this American petty-bourgeois philistine — a real predecessor of H.G. Wells, who lifted several ideas from him, was attaining a wide popularity. It was written, too, shortly after the events of "Bloody Sunday" in Trafalgar Square had given a foretaste of the ferocity of the bourgeoisie — a ferocity displayed many times since up to last month's atrocities in Vienna and always regarded by the myth-mongers and reformists on each occasion as an "accident" in the "peaceful path" to Socialism. It was written fugitively for publication in the weekly *Commonweal*, the organ of the Socialist League (the revival of whose name by the unspeakable Cripps and his crew of faint-hearts is another befoulment of Morris's memory). Just because of its fugitive and unconsidered nature it is possible to estimate Morris's views; because if what a man says in a hastily written series forms an artistic and logical whole, then we can be certain that it represents his essential outlook.

Morris set out in *News from Nowhere* to write a Utopian romance about a Communist Society, about what Marx called the "higher phase" of Communist society, when the State shall have withered away and the Government of Men given way to the Administration of Things. A romance is not to be judged like a treatise, and clearly some of the matters in News from Nowhere are set down by Morris just as they came up his back; and so it is really astonishing the extent to which Morris's picture corresponds to the indications given by Marx in his letter on the "Gotha Programme" and even anticipates some of the features already beginning to show themselves in embryo in the present transition to Socialism within the U.S.S.R.

Those who fail to see the insistence upon the civil war as the central feature of *News from Nowhere*, also blame Morris because, unlike Anatole France, in his *White Stone*, he did not draw a picture of the marvellous machinery of the future society. But since it is precisely the same type of people who omitted to note, in the case of Anatole France, the insistence on the proletarian dictatorship as a preliminary to his future society — and this in a book written ten years before the Russian Revolution — their opinions on Morris can have but little value. Supposing Morris had made his book hum with machines and complicated metal devices, what would have happened? His machines, imagined before the age of electricity, before the age of flying machines, or wireless or television, would have been not the machines of a Communist society, but of a decade, or at most, two decades ahead of 1890. Morris did not care to display the wooden imagination of an H. G. Wells in his *Anticipations*, which would have made his book take on the peculiarly ephemeral quality of Well's pre-war writings. Thus Morris, while missing the local popularity of the man who can tell what the parson is going to have for dinner by virtue of having peeped over the Vicarage wall and seen the Cook plucking mint. Indeed, what Morris says is that the productive forces have enormously developed while as for the actual machines of Communist society, he says that they were beyond his comprehension or capacity to explain.

For Morris was not concerned simply with the improved and novel machinery which he assumed as the basis of heavy industry and transportation, but with the productive relations of men. Given these developed productive powers, his business was to imagine a world with no exploitation of man by man, with no birthmarks of capitalism, or — to give it a local habitation and a name — to picture the lower reaches of the Thames as they would be in the higher phase of Communism. Morris goes on to make one assumption, which is unlikely enough, namely, that after the material basis of Communism is laid there comes to mankind an epoch of rest wherein men express their joy in labour, largely through handicraft. Nevertheless, this assumption of a temporary epoch of rest before the advance of mankind to further heights of Communist development is an essential part of Morris's picture. Once this assumption was made, what else was to be expected but that Morris would hark back to the London as it once was, where "Geoffrey Chaucer's pen moves over bills of lading," to get some concrete idea of what it again might be. So the stones of his buildings seem hewn out of the masonry of the Middle Ages. And the picture recalls the opening lines of his *Earthly Paradise*:

> Forget six counties overhung with smoke
> Forget the snorting steam and piston stroke
> Forget the spreading of the hideous town;
> Think rather of the pack-horse on the down,
> And dream of London, small and white and clean,
> The clear Thames bordered by its gardens green.

There is a prevalent objection to the absorption of Morris in the Middle Ages, an objection partly warranted. For the Middle Ages from which he drew inspiration were also a fetter on his thought. But the objection often goes beyond this and is partly due to the lack of understanding of Utopias and how they are made and imagined. After the Renaissance utopias of Sir Thomas More and Rabelais, the first great outburst of utopian thoughts and imagination were in the writings of the

French revolutionaries, who imagined "justice," "equality" and all other "republican virtues" to be just around the corner. But when they wanted symbols of their dreams they evoked the ancient Republics of Rome and Sparta, the toga and the Phrygian cap. Utopians all look back to a golden age and then project it into the future.

If the ancient world of the slave holders may be used in a transfigured form by other Utopists, then William Morris may evoke John Ball as well as Spartacus, or Chaucer's London instead of Lacedaemon. So presently, in his Utopian romance, some of the atmosphere of the transfigured Middle Ages is built up as the antithesis to the atmosphere of London fifty years ago. But this atmosphere, this fragrance of the Garden of England in which this Communist dialogue is written, so overpoweringly assails the senses already drugged by the Labour-I.L.P. myth, that, seemingly, many who wander there hear the News from Nowhere but do not hearken to it; remember the fragrance of the garden, but nothing of the men who dwelt therein. It is as though readers of the Dialogues of Plato were to remember only their setting — the shady plane tree beyond the banks of the Cephisos and Socrates paddling his feet in the burn, but forget what the Dialogue was about.

We, who can look back over the developing years since Morris wrote, can see with what insight he beheld the class struggle in Europe. Had he lived another ten years he would have seen many features of his chapter on "How the Change Came" enacted in the year 1905 in Russia, from the massacre of Bloody Sunday, through the mutinies of the armed forces and the General Strike to the creation of Soviets (Workers' Committees, Morris called them), the formation of Black hundreds and, finally, the armed rising.

All this does not mean that William Morris had anything like the understanding of Marxism that was afterwards to be shown by the Bolsheviks. On the contrary, he allowed himself to be influenced by the Anarchists, showed an anti-

Parliamentary tendency, and several other similar tendencies — all of them (as Lenin was to note afterwards) a punishment of the movement for the sins of opportunism rampant in Hyndman and the Fabians.

If Maxim Gorki, who may be rightly acclaimed as the greatest artistic force of the Russian proletariat, made mistake after mistake, even in the most serious moments of the Revolution, how much more is this likely to have been so of Morris who had lived four parts of his life before he joined the Social Democratic Federation in his fiftieth year. Just herein lies the contradiction which made it hard for Morris to grasp and apply with full correctness the teachings of Marx.

But these things no more entitle Morris to be canonised as a Reformist by two generations of the Labour Party and I.L.P. than Gorki's weaknesses would entitle him to be regarded as a Whiteguardist and a Menshevik.

It is high time that the Morris myth was destroyed: for the real Morris belongs to us, belongs to the revolutionary working class of Great Britain.

Many this centenary year will be turning to read *News from Nowhere* or *An Epoch of Rest, being some chapters from a Utopian romance*. As they do it they should realise that the poet, once "the idle singer of an empty day" in the 'sixties, had developed by his great period of the 'eighties into the full revolutionary artist.

Why the Disappointed Demagogue Turns to Fascism

LLOYD GEORGE, the well-known British politician, has come out in support of Hitler following on his journey and his interview with the Fuehrer at the time of the Nuremberg Congress. Though both papers in which his views appeared criticized him editorially and though the remainder of the British press for the most part chose to ignore his utterances it would be a mistake to regard this as having no significance.

Their significance depends on the present position of British imperialism, particularly its foreign policy. The center of gravity of the foreign policy of British imperialism at the present moment lies in Europe, in its European policy.

One section of the ruling classes stands for support for France against Hitler but has misgivings as to the French Popular Front. Another section, of which Lord Londonderry was the spokesman, is out and out pro-Hitler; a third section balances between these. General agreement exists only on the policy of rearmament, in regard to which the National Government is now being offered the support of Bevin, Citrine and other reformist leaders.

The pro-Hitler section was formerly the most influential one, and is now more and more supported by the city and the bankers. But this policy is utterly repugnant to the mass of the British people and no one of the pro-Hitler section has been able to make it popular. A vacancy has thus appeared for a new role, namely, that of a pro-Hitlerite, capable by his propaganda, of penetrating among the masses. Here is where Lloyd George steps in.

He announces that there is a "New Germany". He maintains that in this Germany there is no longer any class struggle nor indeed any struggle of any kind. He asserts that this

Germany does not threaten anyone.

Something else however attracted the attention of our traveler in this idyllic Germany.

> "I found everywhere [*i.e.*, among the leaders of Hitlerism—R.P.A.]," he wrote, "a fierce and uncompromising hostility to Russian Bolshevism, coupled with a genuine admiration for the British people, with a profound desire for a better and friendlier understanding with them."

He actually defends the ravings at Nuremberg and has the effrontery to explain the Nuremberg speech and the claims of the Nazis to take the Ukraine as having nothing to do with warlike intentions and that it was merely "a taunt".

Finally, Lloyd George finds the following remarkable explanation of the "recent outbursts against Russia" as being only

> ". . . the common form of diplomatic relationship between Communist Russia and the rest of the world on both sides."

It is nothing more than this, he says, and is not intended as a provocation to war. Again and again he repeats "it does not mean war".

The title of the article of Lloyd George is "I Talk to Hitler". It is more apparent that Hitler talked to him. The utterances of Lloyd George sound like a gramophone record of the familiar Nazi propaganda.

So, in fine, Lloyd George has become Hitler's

mouthpiece for Britain. But he can only become this because Lloyd George long ago in Britain has ceased to be the mouthpiece of any section of the people's opinion.

To those who remember Lloyd George as the radical politician before the war or as the successful War Minister of British imperialism, it may seem strange to learn that Lloyd George has sunk so low in popular esteem, has become so bankrupt that he is now making his last gambler's throw, staking his all on the Knave of Clubs. Yet the fact is that this one-time leading figure of the Liberal Party, this war-time Prime Minister, this all-powerful head of the Liberal-Tory coalition of 1918 to 1922 has lost his support in every political party. The working class hates him, the Tories distrust him, the Liberal Party is split into two sections, neither of which includes Lloyd George.

In Parliament he sits as the chieftain of the Lloyd George Family Party, consisting of himself, his son, his son-in-law and his daughter. So this ruthless, clever, wily, unscrupulous demagogue has reached the position of a political outcast and like other well-known adventurers of the war period, like Ludendorff or Millerand and others, he has steadily sunk in the general esteem. Recognizing this, he has now decided to stake his all, and to risk a desperate course.

Lenin already characterized Lloyd George with keen insight in 1916, when he wrote:

> "A first-class bourgeois business man and master of political cunning, a popular orator, able to make any kind of speech, even r-r-revolutionary speeches before labor audiences, capable of securing fairly considerable sops for the obedient workers in the shape of social reforms (insurance, etc.)—Lloyd George serves the bourgeoisie splendidly. He serves it precisely among the workers, he transmits its influence precisely to the

proletariat, where it is most necessary and most difficult morally to subjugate the masses."

Notice that what was demagogy, flattery, lies and fraud before the war, in a word Lloyd George-ism, now finds its easy affinity and historic development in this friendship with Hitler and Hitlerite fascism. But Lloyd George has also been a practitioner of the other side of fascism, of its brutal suppression of the exploited and oppressed, its bestial cruelty, its politics of murder. It was Lloyd George who was responsible Prime Minister in the suppression of the Indian masses in 1919 to 1922 in the first great struggle for liberation, when hundreds were mowed down by machine-guns in the massacre at Jallianwala Bagh (Amritsar) and when the atrocity of the Mopleh death train horrified the world. He was directly and personally responsible for the Black and Tans in Ireland, the fascist gangs whose deeds of robbery, arson, rape and murder outdid the worst minions of Castlereagh2 and set a model for the subsequent infamies of the Hitler Blackshirts. It was Lloyd George who was personally responsible for allowing the Irish rebel Terence McSweeney, the Lord Mayor of Cork, on hunger strike in an English dungeon, to starve to a lingering death.

Already at Versailles, in 1919, Lloyd George was outstanding in his fear of revolution. For him, it was a case of "Bolshevisme, voila l'emlemi"! He operated this standpoint through all vicissitudes of Anglo-Soviet trade agreements, enmities with France, Washington treaties, and the Genoa conference. Social insurance as introduced by him in 1911 was, as he himself has explained, not an insurance for the working class against sickness, etc., so much as an insurance for the bourgeoisie, insurance against revolution. Lenin, writing in 1920, quotes Lloyd George's speech of March 18, 1920, in which he said:

"... . civilization is in danger. ... This country is more top-heavy than any country in the world and if it begins to rock, the crash here for that reason will be greater than in any land."

On which Lenin comments:

"The reader will see that Lloyd George is not only a clever man, but that he has also learned a great deal from the Marxists."

Consistent only in one thing, in his hatred of revolution, this adventurer who has boxed the compass of politics rallied to the support of Hitler fascism, at a moment when all other English politicians were speaking against Hitler and Nazism. On September 22, 1933, Lloyd George declared in a speech at Barmouth:

"If the Powers succeed in overthrowing Nazism in Germany, what would follow? Not a Conservative, Socialist or Liberal regime, but extreme Communism. Surely that could not be their objective. A Communist Germany would be infinitely more formidable than a Communist Russia."

And again in the House of Commons on November 28, 1934, when even the Tory press and politicians were voicing anti-Nazi sentiments following on the Roehm-Von Schleicher murders, Lloyd George said:

"In a very short time, perhaps in a year or two,

the Conservative elements in this country will be looking to Germany as the bulwark against Communism in Europe. She is planted right in the center of Europe, and if Germany is seized by the Communists, Europe will follow; because the Germans could make a better job of it than any other country. Do not let us be in a hurry to condemn Germany. We shall be welcoming Germany as our friend."

And now, at a moment when the reformist leaders in Britain are vilifying the Soviet Union and Communism so as to prevent a united front in Britain, Lloyd George has chosen to come out with the utmost openness as the defender and mouthpiece of Hitler. For several years past, using his talents as orator, writer and matchless intriguer, Lloyd George has sought to get back into power. If he cannot get one way, if the people reject him, then he will find another way, he thinks.

It was not difficult for Lloyd George to admire Hitler. In 1920, it was being currently reported in England that Lloyd George kept voicing this sentiment "what this country want is a dictator, a Caesar". But it is not only in foreign affairs that Lloyd George wishes to be allied with Hitler. In home affairs he goes in the same direction. In January, 1935, his "new deal" program of unemployment and reconstruction was a bid for popular support. In this he failed. But it received a welcome from fascist quarters. Lord Londonderry, then head of the Air Force, chief supporter of Hitler in the National Government, said:

"Mr. Lloyd George put forward a constructive plan, and I am glad to hear that the Chancellor of the Exchequer proposed to look carefully into it. . . ."

The *Daily Mail*, with its fascist proclivities, said:

"For all these proposals he will find abundant support. He is a great enterprise well begun, and his lead will be followed the more eagerly because he declares definitely against the wild gentry who would nationalize the joint stock banks or, in plain English, rob the community."

The *Blackshirt*, organ of Sir Oswald Mosley, called the speech "the first step on the road to fascist conclusions".

In the last two years Lloyd George has been writing a history of the war of 1914-1918. Of this history he is the "hero". In it he appears as the "revolutionary" (in the Nazi sense of the word), struggling against incompetent generals, politicians, traitors and vested interests. It is not surprising that the author of this English version of *Mein Kampf* should be a friend of Hitler.

If Lloyd George has cast himself for the role of Hitler's friend in the present situation in Britain, it is of course not out of love for Lord Londonderry or Neville Chamberlain or Ramsay MacDonald or any other pro-Hitlerites, though he really serves their present purpose well. Lloyd George is doing it for his own purpose. What are his calculations? He is speculating on the love for peace that is widespread among the English masses who hate war and who hate the aggressor. To the masses he says in effect, "the British people must have peace, neither the National Government nor the Labor Party can guarantee peace. I am 'the man who won the war'. I am also the man who can win the peace. Trust me. I can make a friend of Hitler. Hitler is no aggressor. Trust me—in the *name of peace*".

But so far the masses have not been deceived. The vast majority of letters which poured into the *News Chronicle* attacked Lloyd George. One of them stated clearly that "Mr. Lloyd George wants British democracy united with German fascism against not the menace but the triumph of Marxism in the U.S.S.R.". Lloyd George's fellow Liberal, Eleanor Rathbone, M.P., gave him a sharp rebuff in the *Manchester Guardian*, and finally threatened a schism in the Liberal-pacifist organization called the Council of Action if Lloyd George is supported by any other Liberals or religious leaders.

The result was immediate. Lloyd George was forced to publish a rejoiner to his critics in which he claimed that his only or main object had been to arouse the democracy of Britain to deal with unemployment, ill health and bad conditions as effectively as had been done in Soviet Russia, or (!) as had been done, as he, Lloyd George, asserts, in Hitler Germany. Thus in his reply he falls back on the attempt to confuse the masses by bracketing the U.S.S.R. with the bestialities of Hitler fascism, and by representing himself as consumed with love for democracy.

The last attempt of this disappointed demagogue, Lloyd George, to stage a comeback may end in his final extinction as a political figure ,but only if the attack is pushed home by every one of those who are against the menace of war and the danger of fascism.

Since this was written, Lloyd George has suddenly (in an interview in "Reynolds", October 4, 1936) announced himself as a supporter of a Popular Front in Britain.

But this maneuver has only to be closely examined for its disgusting fascist features to be exposed. He retracts nothing of his praise of Hitler fascism. He makes no mention of the existence of the Communists, even when quoting the example of the People's Front in France, cunningly passing over the Communists. He says that England needs a "Social ideal", like Hitler's.

He abuses the Labor and Liberal Parties, and calls on the discontented masses to rally around himself, Lloyd George, as the Fuehrer of a "Popular Front".

In a word, he wants to drag fascism, into England behind the popular sign of the "People's Front".

We may remind the old demagogue of an episode in English history, when Charles II, warned by his universally detested brother and heir to the throne of a treasonable conspiracy, replied, wittily enough, "James, James, they will never kill me to make you King"! The masses of Britain may be discontented with the present leadership of the Labor Party, but they will never throw it over to make Lloyd George their Fuehrer.

The British Trade Union Congress

THE British Trade Union Congress, which met in Plymouth in the second week of September, was concerned with three main questions, overshadowing all others. These questions were Spain, unity and the unemployed. On all three the reformist leadership (Bevin, Citrine, etc.), had a measure of success, but under such circumstances as may easily render that success negatory.

To understand these circumstances it is necessary to recall the fact that nine months ago the reformist leadership were not only the chief obstacle to working class unity internationally, but inside Britain regarded their policy against unity as secure and unchallenged. The campaign of the Communist Party for affiliation to the Labor Party, in furtherance of the decisions of the Seventh World Congress, they regarded with contempt. They formally rejected the application and maintained a lofty silence, disdaining to engage in controversy.

But as the campaign for affiliation developed, as more and more working class organizations supported the Communists, they changed from aloofness to chagrin. When the victories of the Popular Front in Spain and in France, followed by the enormous gains of the French working class won by great strikes and through a unified trade union movement, gave an enormous impetus to the movement for unity in Britain, the chagrin of the reformist leaders changed to alarm.

And they had something about which to be alarmed, namely: the workers in the British factories were eagerly discussing and saying: "What they have done in France, we could do in Britain". Among the British intellectuals and radical lower middle class there began to be discussions of the Popular Front, and not only trade unions but the Socialist societies, the most active ideologically of the constituent parts of the Labor

Party, became partisans of unity, while even the Fabian Society, for well-nigh thirty years the chief ideological guide of the Labor movement, decided to support Communist affiliation.

In reply to this, the reformist leaders in the middle of June launched a most vicious counter-campaign against unity, employing all the resources of their speakers, press and other publications. The attack on unity was twofold. In the first place they attacked the Communist Party of Great Britain, raking up all the familiar fascist arguments about "Moscow gold", etc. In the second place they delivered a frontal attack on the Soviet Union whose prestige and popularity among the masses of Britain they felt to be dangerous to their own policy. The new Soviet Constitution was first attacked. Then, Sir Walter Citrine's book against the U.S.S.R. was published. Then the blackest portions of this book were reprinted as a series of articles in the *Daily Herald* which from that time until now has conducted an unceasing campaign against the U.S.S.R. But with all this the reformist leaders were unable to prevent the Miners' Federation of Great Britain (half a million members) from supporting Communist affiliation.

The fascist rebellion in Spain caused a further change.

The reactionary press were against giving help to the people of Spain. The Liberal, Labor and Communist press supported the Spanish people. The masses of Britain began to be aroused.

The reformist leaders of the trade unions (Bevin, Citrine, etc.), at the beginning compelled to pronounce themselves for Spain and to open a fund, now beheld with dismay the current for unity rapidly becoming a tide.

The events developing in Spain sharpened more and more the mood of the class struggle, to the detriment of their policy of class collaboration. Unless they could break the rapidly growing front for unity, nationally and internationally, their policy was doomed to defeat. So far they had been able to maintain as regards Spain, the standpoint of "neutrality". But that might not last. To achieve their ends, they must come out still more openly. The notorious telegram defending the Trotsky-Zinoviev Terrorist Center was dispatched by Citrine, de Brouckere, Schevenels and Adler. Together with the whole bourgeois press, the reformist leaders solidarized themselves with the fascist attack on the U.S.S.R.

These were the circumstances in which the Trade Union Congress met at Plymouth. In their policy of "neutrality" as regards Spain, *i.e.*, a policy of support for the line of the British Foreign Office, Bevin and Citrine were able to win support for the National Council of Labor. They were only able to do this by the use of unscrupulous demagogy, by presenting the matter in such terms as made it seem a condemnation of the National Government, by pleading that any other decision would mean the downfall of the Blum government (!), by making false statements against the British Communist Party and the French Communist Party by suggesting that to give the Spanish government assistance would immediately unloose a European war.

In spite of all this, there were big oppositional minorities inside the industrial delegations, especially the miners; and the railwaymen finally withheld their vote. Even so, Herbert Morrison, the reformist leader of the London Labor Party, has gone so far as to break the discipline of the Labor Party, saying on September 5:

> "I cannot reconcile myself to this 'neutrality' business. It is so unjust, so unfair to a people heroically fighting against heavy and cruel odds."

Morrison would not, of course, do this unless he felt he had the support of a large minority of delegates which, depending on the further development of the Spanish events, might turn into a majority at the Labor Party Conference.

At Sheffield on September 13, Sir Charles Trevelyan, Labor ex-Minister, said:

> "I regard it at this moment as a disaster that the Labor movement should have fallen into the trap of feebleness prepared by the British government."

That this statement more truly represents the mass of the British workers than the T.U.C. decisions is also shown by the tremendous demonstrations held by the Communist Party in London on September 6 and 20. On September 6, £700, the largest open-air collection ever taken in Britain in working class history, was raised for the Spanish people; and the London correspondent of the Swedish Social-Democratic paper, *Arbetet* (Malmo), who has no reason to favor the Communists, writes on September 16:

> "At the moment it seems almost as if the British Communist Party had seized the initiative when it was a question of giving expression to the deep unrest in Liberal circles and in the Labor movement in Great Britain over the policy of non-interference in Spain. . . . The initiative, which the Communist Party appeared to have seized in this business, is now beginning to produce considerable discomfort in the organized Labor movement of Great Britain. . . ."

In the week preceding the Congress the *Daily Herald*, organ of Bevin and Citrine, had outdone the fascist *Daily Mail* in its dissemination of lies with regard to the Soviet Union. Nevertheless it was sufficient to defeat the proposal, sponsored by the Amalgamated Engineering Union and other important unions, to send an official delegation to the Soviet Union. On the other hand, the general resolution for international trade union unity was carried without opposition, since at the London Triennial Conference of the International Federation of Trade Unions in July, a similar resolution had already been carried. But Sir Walter Citrine immediately after the T.U.C. chose to interpret these resolutions as enabling him first of all to approach the American Federation of Labor.

On unemployment, the proposal was brought forward for a hunger march on London, for a boycott of the coronation festivities and a one-day industrial strike. In successfully opposing this Sir Walter Citrine used arguments—"against industrial and other action" which might well have been voiced by Baldwin. But then, it has to be remembered that, as in medieval times, a knight bears special allegiance to his liege lord and must do extraordinary deeds—or find extraordinary arguments, as in this case.

On immediate economic issues, the reformist leaders offered no opposition, or even supported the resolutions brought forward. Resolutions were carried demanding a 40-hour week, holidays with pay, and an all-inclusive scheme of social insurance. To press these through in face of any sabotage by the leaders now becomes a task of militant workers in Britain.

The passage of these resolutions reveals very clearly the cunning tactics adopted by the reformist leaders (with what help from even more skilled tacticians of class struggle in Downing Street or the City must remain unknown).

While giving ground on the immediate economic demands that stir the working class, they chose the issues of "foreign policy", that lay outside the daily life or the delegates.

They laid their plans well in advance first by their campaign of against the U.S.S.R., and secondly by giving great publicity to the preparatory resolutions of the National Council of Labor, framed to make a pro-Baldwin policy appear as a heavy attack on Baldwin.

Sir Walter Citrine has little to learn in the art of demagogy from Lloyd George or Lloyd George's friend, the Nazis.

Nevertheless, the situation does not permit the reformists to rest secure for another year. That they understand this is clear from the choice of Bevin (the power behind the throne of Citrine) as the new chairman of the Trades Union Congress.

There are such meetings now in Britain as never before in aid of the masses of another country. The tide of popular feeling has not been stemmed by the decisions of the Trades Union Congress. The campaign for unity in the fight against war and fascism is gathering strength among the masses, as one after another the false statements of the T.U.C. leaders are exposed, as the example of the Soviet Union inspires the peoples of Britain; as the need for action grows manifestly more urgent every day. While the reformists who supported the National Government on Ethiopia last year, and now on Spain, are turning to support it on armaments, the revolt of the masses will grow greater. The Citrine "victory" or the T.U.C. may well begin a differentiation between those who feel the pleasure of big business and those who feel the pressure of big masses.

The Struggle for Unity in Great Britain

AT THE celebration of the twentieth anniversary of the great proletarian revolution, British workers not only rejoice at the present achievements and the future glorious prospects of the Soviet Union, but also cast their minds back over the past twenty years and see the stupendous contrast, not only with what was under tsardom but with what was and is in Great Britain now. Here was a backward country, its agriculture primitive, its population largely illiterate, its working class and peasantry deprived of rights: here on the other hand was one of the most advanced countries of the world, its population literate, with its working class for well-nigh a century organized and enjoying a measure of democratic rights won in struggle. And now? Which is advanced and which is backward?

Of all the contrasts which are vividly present to the mind of the British working class at this moment the most poignant is the contrast between the single united party of the working class, the Communist Party of the Soviet Union (the Bolsheviks) and the disunited conditions of the British labor movement. The existence of the monolithic Party of the U.S.S.R. is the clue to the triumph now being celebrated. The disunity in British labor is the clue to its continued subjection to the handful of millionaires who are the real owners of the British National government.

The British Prime Minister, Neville Chamberlain, has been boasting that his government is stronger than ever before——but its apparent strength resides solely in the weakness and confusion of the opposition to it. There is no real strength in the position of the British bourgeoisie. On the contrary the might of British imperialism, already on the wane since the general crisis of capitalism, has been still further eclipsed by the military aggression of German-Italian-Japanese fascism threatening its trade routes, its Empire connections and its dominating position in the markets of the world. This has had an effect on all parties and classes, causing confusion, shiftings, differentiation. The effects of the world economic crisis have had a lasting impression. Not only the working class, but those intermediate sections of the population, such as small businessmen, farmers and professionals have felt the adverse effects of the crisis, and have been seeking some means of escape from the difficult position into which they have been thrust. The speed-up and increased accidents in the workshops, the fall in real wages, the alarming extent of malnutrition are paralleled amongst the intermediate sections by the rise in prices, professional unemployment, uncertainty for the future, while the whole people stand under the shadow of the menace of war and fascism.

Here is the opportunity for the working class of Great Britain, with its tradition of organization, with its history of struggle reaching back to the Chartists, to lead in organizing and rallying the whole people, but the chief labor organizations of Great Britain, in just this period of the opportunity and the crying need for unity, are headed by such reactionary leaders as Ernest Bevin and Sir Walter Citrine, who have done everything to bring about disunity in the labor movement to the advantage of no one but the capitalists.

The recent Labor Party Conference has given a signal that it is becoming more and more difficult for Bevin-Citrine and Co. to carry through this policy of disunity. The point is that ever since the Seventh Congress of the Communist International the issues have been sharply joined, but especially in the last fifteen months the conflict between the policy of unity in the fight against fascism, reaction and war, on the one hand, and the policy of disunity, with covert or open support of the millionaires and their National government on the other hand, has become sharper and sharper. The more the line of the Seventh Congress of the Communist International came to be understood and applied by masses of workers in the trade unions, the more fiercely have the Bevin-Citrine group fought to destroy the building of unity.

To bring about disunity, both on a national and international scale, they launched a foul, lying campaign against the U.S.S.R. with Citrine's book, and took under their protection the Trotskyite spies and terrorists who had been brought to trial before the court of the working people of the U.S.S.R. This anti-Soviet campaign continues up to this moment. Within the British trade unions they sought to exterminate the influence of the Communists; after the London bus strike of May, 1937, the strike leaders were expelled from the union.

With a bitterness which aroused comment in the capitalist press they fought against the unity campaign and threatened with expulsion and excommunication Stafford Cripps, who led the campaign inside the Labor Party. They prevented help being given to Spain, supported the Franco-helping non-intervention policy of the National government and in this way played into the hands of this government. They hamstrung their own parliamentary Labor Party, when, this summer, it wanted to vote down war credits and, as a token of their real support of the 1,500 million pounds arms policy of the National government, insisted on a policy of abstention from voting.

The leadership of the labor movement of Britain had proved unable to rally the workers for the struggle against the policy of the National government. The critical situation was driving forward the process of differentiation within the Labor Party. Not only the Left wing headed by Cripps, which had been fighting for the affiliation of the Communist Party of Great Britain to the Labor Party, stood out clearly but a large center grouping, represented by Attlee and others, opposed the reactionary leaders. For a time all that the Right wing did in face of this was to drive ahead more viciously with its splitting policy.

But meantime there were new circumstances which

prevented the carrying out to the full their splitting plans and compelled the Right wing to maneuver. First of all, the invasion of the Basque territory, the destruction of Guernica and Bilbao had aroused a real wave of popular indignation in Britain for the first time since the fascist rebellion and invasion of Spain began. In July there was a definite outspoken opposition in Parliament to the National government policy comprising Labor and Liberal M.P.'s and Lloyd George.

Second, despite the measures taken to cripple the unity campaign it was clear that the demand for unity had met with a very wide response amongst the workers, who remained cold to the efforts of the leadership to present the Labor Party as itself being the "one and only" united front.

Third, the obvious setback to the Labor Party throughout the country, caused by the Bevin-Citrine policy and the apparent unlikelihood of an early Labor government, had led to a demand for a wider grouping in support of democracy and peace, for help to Spain and for collective security. This demand which the Trade Union Congress had rejected in September, 1936, that the people of Britain should emulate the successes of the People's Front in France, began once more to be put forward and was voiced by many Labor and Liberal intellectuals.

Fourth, the extremely rapid rise in the cost of living, together with the worsening of workshop conditions, was accompanied by new rising mass pressure for increases in wages, for shorter hours; for labor holidays with pay, etc. The defeat of the bus strike in London had only a temporary effect and the new mass pressure showed itself first in the novel form of strikes of apprentices, especially in the war industry.

Under all these circumstances, with the approach of the Trade Union Congress in September and the Labor Party Conference in October, the Bevin-Citrine leadership planned its maneuver as follows:

1. To avoid a struggle at the Trades Union Congress by yielding on the question of Spain and by sundry "Left" gestures and resolutions.

2. To gag the Labor Party Conference by ruling out from the agenda all resolutions on unity.

3. To commit both these annual gatherings to implicit support of the government arms program.

How did the maneuver succeed? At the Trades Union Congress it was successful; at the Labor Party Conference the Bevin-Citrine group, while winning on the question of arms and unity, were severely defeated on inner-party democracy and on the elections to the Executive. The Labor Party Conference represents a defeat that seriously impairs the success of the whole maneuver.

At the Trades Union Congress, Bevin and Citrine seemed to have it all their own way. On Spain, these Right-wing leaders who had sabotaged the fight of the Spanish people, who in the Second International had prevented international working class united action, now came forward to denounce the "nonintervention" policy for which they are utterly responsible —with the result that their critics were compelled to vote for the resolution proposed by Sir Walter Citrine.

Actually, this yielding on Spain, China on economic questions, was made possible by the fighting mood of the working class, and, accordingly, in those resolutions a basis is given for the Communist Party to lead a struggle for the putting into effect of these results of the Trades Union Congress.

At the Labor Party Conference, on the issues chosen for debate, they appeared to be equally successful. Unity had been ruled out of discussion. The question could only arise by referring back the Executive's report—a procedure which weighs the odds against any change because it must take the form of a condemnation, in this respect, of the elected executive.

On the question of arms, they managed to avoid the issue being prominently raised for or against the National government. The debate was chiefly with the pacifists. While the Lansbury section was correctly defeated by the Centrist speakers for collective security, the fact that the Labor Party had been implicitly permitted to support the National government was underlined by the outspoken jingo utterances of the 1914 social-chauvinist vein of several speakers.

But this apparent success was robbed of its value by the decision of the local Labor Parties and by the election of new forces standing for working class unity. The local Labor Parties, dissatisfied for years with the domination of the powerful trade unions, had demanded larger representation in the Executive Committee. The Executive had conceded an increase from five to seven, making the total number 25. At the conference, Bevin, Marchbanks, Secretary for Railwaymen, and other Right wingers opposed this extension of democratic rights, including the choice of their representatives directly by the local Labor Parties. They were defeated. Further, the local Labor Parties made use of their newly-won rights to elect to the Executive as their representatives, Cripps (leader of the campaign for unity within the Labor Party), Laski and Pritt. This was a still more serious defeat.

The *Daily Herald*, together with the *Manchester Guardian*, tried to make light of this result which they presented as evidence of the magnanimity and brotherly-love spirit of the Labor leaders. But the fact was that the representatives of the local Labor Parties, though by no means all of them Left in their outlook, are seriously alarmed by the situation of the Labor Party. The meetings in the recent campaign for 100,000 new members have been miserably poor, and a strong contrast to the large and enthusiastic meetings addressed by Cripps and by the leaders of the Communist Party.

Well might the Times print a rueful editorial, headed

"Labor Looks Left," for the happy mood which the Trade Union Congress had brought to the Times as well as to Messrs. Bevin and Citrine had been rudely disturbed:

> "The Labor Party Conference last week accepted a demand for a bolder and more aggressive leadership; a more thorough and uncompromising presentation of the socialist creed; an open recognition and vigorous conduct of class war. No such resolution will appear on the records of the conference, but it is written in the reconstruction of the Executive Committee and in the high spirits and rejoicings of the representatives of the constituency Labor parties. . . .
>
> "But there were deeds as well as words, elections as well as resolutions, and the Executive that now directs the affairs of the Party is not the old Executive, for it includes the two forceful freelances whom the old Executive was threatening with expulsion from the Party —Sir Stafford Cripps and Professor Laski—and with them stands Mr. D. N. Pritt. The principal champion of the 'united front,' the most persistent advocate of the class war in the party, has been set by constituency party votes on the party's governing body."

It is clear enough from this that these results of the Labor Party Conference have caused dismay among the bourgeoisie. Despite the reactionary decisions on unity and on the arms policy of the National government, this Bournemouth Labor Party Conference signifies a considerable change in the working class from last year.

But the change as yet is mainly in the possibilities it opens up of renewed struggle, by the whole people of Britain against reaction, fascism and war. To make these possibilities now opened up into actualities, to turn the resolutions on China and Spain, on foreign policy and home affairs into an effective mass movement, require the utmost persistence and a determined struggle.

The Central Committee of the Communist Party of Great Britain which before the Bournemouth Conference had issued an appeal to the delegates to rise to the height of the opportunity offered to labor to give a lead to the whole mass of the people, published an important statement following the Conference in which it was said:

"The more effectively the Labor Party is organized to fight against rising prices and profits; the stronger its demand for higher wages and shorter hours, and against encroachments on democratic rights; for solidarity with the Spanish and Chinese peoples in their heroic struggles against fascism; for unity of action against fascist aggression on the part of all democratic states identified with the League of Nations, and for independent working class action to force the National government to carry out the demands of labor immediately—the greater will be the possibilities for the development of a mass movement of all working class and progressive people of Britain."

But for this purpose, and for the defeat of the National government, working class unity is essential. Therefore, the Communist Party of Great Britain in this statement once again expressed "its readiness to become affiliated to the Labor Party" and said:

"We wish to overcome the difficulties which have hitherto prevented cooperation between the Labor Party and the Communist Party in the struggle against capitalism and the National government.

"The Communist Party accepts in its full meaning the Constitution of the Labor Party, it will abide by all decisions of Labor Party Conferences; it will not ask for special privileges and will accept the same obligations and rights as all other affiliated organizations to the Labor Party."

It dealt with the various objections raised to Communist affiliation and stated that:

"The Communist Party in all earnestness and seriousness declares its readiness to discuss with representatives of the Labor Party the objections that they may feel stand in the way of the achievement of working class unity."

It is clear that unless unity of the working class is brought about, unless all progressive and democratic forces in Britain are rallied, the danger of fascism and of war will increase still more rapidly. But if the struggle is waged effectively to carry out this struggle for unity, including affiliation of the Communist Party to the Labor Party, then around a united working class movement there can be such a rallying of progressive and democratic forces as will force a change now in the policy of the National government. Such a movement can replace the National government by a government carrying through a policy of democracy at home and abroad.

The Communist Party and the Colonies

One of the greatest obstacles to the emancipation of the British working class has been the fetters that tied it to the Empire, the identification of its interests with those of the imperialist ruling class. One of the greatest weaknesses of the Socialist Parties of Europe was found in their attitude to the national question; which in the question of the colonies became particularly obvious. From this it has been the task of the Communist Party of Great Britain and of the Communist International to rescue the labour movement of Britain and of the other countries.

Already, in the nineteenth century, Marx said of England's oldest colony – Ireland – that a nation which oppresses others cannot itself be free. Later, Engels was pointing out the effect of Britain's monopoly of the world market and the colonial market upon the British labour movement, but at the same time prophesying that once the colonial monopoly was broken the working-class movement would develop.

With the development of imperialism, the latest stage of capitalism, in the twentieth century, the ruling class, from its super-profits of colonial exploitation, was able to spare crumbs to the upper section of the labour movement; and their representatives, the reformist right-wing leaders, began to argue on behalf of the maintenance and extension of the whole Empire system of exploitation.

In 1900 Bernard Shaw wrote his booklet *Fabianism and the Empire* in which the policy of the ruling class in the South African war of 1899-1902 was justified. The German Social-Democrats, a little later, began to argue that since European powers like Germany were so much more advanced in capitalist development than the states of Asia or Africa, therefore the extension of the colonial plunder of the big powers was actually an 'advance'.

Against this, in 1907 at the Stuttgart International Socialist Congress, the left wing of the International were able to defeat those, including Ramsay MacDonald, who wished to recognise the 'civilising mission' of capitalism. But so insidious was the influence of the reformists that nearly 20 years later one of the followers of Ramsay MacDonald, the Rt Hon Tom Johnston, ignorantly arguing in the public press that while he agreed with the Stuttgart resolution, he nevertheless interpreted it to mean the maintenance of the British Empire as a political power for good. So that the more clear it was that one end of the chain of imperialism was laid upon the people of this country, the more efforts were made by the reformists to gild the chain and to claim that it was not a chain of slavery but a bond of amity, justice and what not.

Against this degradation of the labour movement, against this perversion of Socialism into support of imperialism, the Communist Party of Great Britain has fought from its very beginning. It has put forward the teachings of Marx and Engels as developed in the era of imperialism by Lenin and by Stalin (whose writings on Marxism and the national and colonial questions have been circulated mainly by Communists), and has steadfastly fought against the poison of opportunism, and of White chauvinism inside the labour movement. In this it had a tremendous task and was not immune from mistakes: but the error made in 1927-28 in not realising that imperialism always treats colonies as an agrarian appendage and never forwards their industrialisation, was speedily corrected with the help of other parties at the Sixth World Congress in 1928, the correctness of whose thesis, drafted by OV Kuusinen, was confirmed a hundred times by the facts given in RP Dutt's *India Today* published a few months ago.

But the struggle of the party for the very soul of the

British working class was shown from the earliest.

In the resolution to the Sixth Party Congress in 1924 it stated:

The Communist Party in conference assembled greets the workers and labouring masses throughout the colonies and dependencies of Great Britain now struggling for freedom and independence. Their cause is our cause. The division amongst the oppressed masses is a source of power to the oppressors. Only the united forces of the enslaved masses of the colonies and dependencies with the wage slaves of Great Britain can secure victory...

This Congress, therefore, renews its pledges of solidarity with the struggling colonial workers and promises the fullest possible assistance in the development of their struggle for freedom. It appreciates it as an immediate duty to denounce and expose the treacherous conduct of the Labour Government in this country. This government has since its accession to office not merely allowed but actually excused and condoned the shooting down and massacre of colonial workers. Thousands of workers are in gaol in Egypt and India and the Labour Government does nothing. Not only that, the Labour Government actually initiates the persecution of the pioneers of Communism in India and Egypt, in order to make the Communist Party in India and Egypt illegal. The Congress sends its fraternal greetings to those workers in gaol and struggling to set up a working-class movement in the colonies, and pledges itself to render every possible assistance in their work.

In these last ten years the differences within the Second

International between the reformist right wing, corrupted by imperialism, and the left wing, the revolutionary Socialists, representing the true interests of the working class, is now clearly seen in practice. On the one side, the Labour Government of 1929-31, keeping the trade-union leaders of India fast in their Meerut gaol, savagely repressing the great wave of Indian struggle in 1930-31, and since, as a tame opposition, saying ditto to the proposals of Tory politicians, so that everyone knows there is no difference for the colonial peoples between the Labour Party and the Tories in practice.

The culmination is that, when Labour representatives are well inside the Churchill government, then it becomes possible to try 'appeasement' on Japan and to institute 'non-intervention' against the Chinese people.

On the other hand, look at the victory of scientific Socialism, of the Marxist-Leninist solution of the national-colonial question. The liberated nationalities that are joining the Soviet Union, the colonial peoples whose culture in the Socialist content and national shape is leaping forward by centuries in a single decade, holding out an inspiration to the mass of mankind, and showing the path to be followed.

See the growth of Communist Parties in the colonies and movements for national liberation. In the record of the Communist Party of Great Britain, in its growing influence on the British labour movement, lies the hope of a successful common struggle of the colonial masses and the British working class against the common enemy, the ruling class of the British Empire.

India Today

The Viceroy, on August 8th, once more offered to sell a pig in a poke to the people of India. There were no buyers. The Indian National Congress which, at the 1937 elections, despite the restricted electorate and heavily rigged arrangements for privileged constituencies, nevertheless obtained at overwhelming majority, is not so easily to be duped. Indeed, the British Government, which authorised the Viceroy to make his statement, can hardly have expected to get from India any response, apart from the ready applause of its own clients and confidants: Nor can they have been altogether surprised when the Muslim president of the Indian National Congress Manlana Kalam Asad, coldly declined to enter the game. From the impudent opening claim that "India's anxiety at this moment of critical importance in the world struggle against tyranny and aggression to contribute to the full to the common cause and to the triumph of our common ideas is manifest" to the flowery statement of "the intentions of His Majesty's Government" the device was altogether too transparent. These intentions turn out to be reiteration of the "full weight" which British Imperialism will lend to and minority to thwart the decisions of the majority of the Indian people; the "revision" (which may mean on the precedent of the Simon Commission either extension or restriction) of the present "constitution" by some third and presumably hand-picked Round Table—provided always that safeguards are maintained for and by the British Imperialists; and that in any case this must all be put off till after the war. Negatively, this means the rejection of the Congress demands for unequivocal recognition of national independence, for self-determination, for the future of India to be decided by a democratically elected Constituent Assembly, and for immediate setting up of a National Government with ministers responsible to elected bodies. The Indian National Congress in the last ten months had asked the British Government to define its intentions towards India: in order that the Indians might judge of the claim that this war was being waged for democracy and freedom. Through the mouth of the Viceroy the reply is hereby given and the Congress leaders are now invited to behave like their predecessors in the war of 1914-18, in return for which they are informed that the principle of "divide and rule" will continue to be operated, that they had better drop their present programme, and that they would do well to accept a post-dated cheque for a new constitutional scheme, "after the war."

In these circumstances, the reason for the Viceroy's statement, followed by the parliamentary debate of August 15th, must be looked upon as the preparation of public opinion at home and in the U.S.A. for the further steps the Government will take to deal with the Congress and the whole liberation movement of the Indian people. Already there have been many arrests, especially of leaders of the Indian working class: and new repressive ordinances (*e.g.* against defence volunteers) have been issued. Moreover, as Jawaharlal Nehru stated in a recent telegram, the closing of the Burma Road to China (with other steps for the appeasement of Japanese Imperialism), is directly opposed to the interests of the Indian people, who have expressed their solidarity with the people of China. Talk of "common ideals" cannot hide this conflict of interests; and in it there lies a threat for the future. But British public opinion, as voiced in the press, as well as the debate in Parliament, appeared to accept without question the Government statements. The press telegrams to India will say that there is "unanimity" behind the Government and the possibility of friendship between the peoples of Britain and India that could develop from an acceptance of the Congress programme will be made more remote. This is a prospect full of peril for the people of this country: and the sooner there is an awakening to this danger and a widespread understanding of India to-day, the sooner the working class and the people of this country will be in a position to solve their own problems.

Precisely at this time the publication of R. Palme Dutt's book on India gives everyone the opportunity of acquiring a full understanding, a criterion by which to judge vice-regal statements and an equipment for participating in the struggle for Colonial liberation, as part of the real "common cause" of the working class and the oppressed peoples against Imperialism.

India To-day is the most important book about it since the time the peoples of India first became subject to the domination of the British capitalists.

It is the best book written in this country on the Colonial Question. It is a profound Marxist study that lays bear the working of Imperialism.

So far, its reception at the hands of reviewers in the Capitalist press has been in inverse proportion to its importance. Handed out to the readers of the Left Book Club on a pair of tongs by Professor Laski, the ideologist of the Labour Party Executive Committee (odd resemblance between the churchmen who "edited" Gibbon to minimise the damage his history might do to their altars and Laski's careful attempt at "decontamination" in the Left News) it has since—apart from one or two hostile notices—received scarcely a single serious review. Under the circumstances of the present war, threatening to involve the whole of mankind, it is noteworthy that the best Marxist work in Western Europe for many a year should be met by a conspiracy of silence. All the more then the working class of the English-speaking countries should make up their minds to get this book and equip themselves from it.

The book falls into five main parts, together with a preliminary chapter on India in the War and a sixth part drawing conclusions as to the future. In Part I, *India as it Is and as it Might Be*, there is presented the problem of India, the 370,000,000 human beings, living in extreme poverty, under a foreign rule which maintains by force the social system, and struggling for the means of life, for elementary freedom. The facts are those admitted by Imperialists that "after two centuries

107

of imperialist rule, India presents a spectacle of squalid poverty and misery of the mass of the people without equal in the world". Nor is it deficiency of resources that explains this; nor long-lasting historic backwardness (for up till the British capitalists came, India was relatively advanced in the world scale of technical development); nor any other specious reason. Citations from imperialist apologists themselves lead to the conclusion that "it is this failure to develop the productive resources of India that finally sounds the death-knell of imperialism in India to-day"; and the necessary transformation, depending on the national movement, on the working masses and especially on the young working class, while having as its first objective the liberation from Imperialism, has then the further issue of the ending of poverty. Before this can be set forth in full, there are necessary sections dealing with the "Silent censorship" over India and the mythologies ("White Man's burden" in all keys) conjured up by the imperialists and spread by them in this country through every agency of propaganda. In Chapter 3 the terrible paradox of the wealth of India and the poverty of India is followed by a complete exposure of the over-population fallacies, the fantastic nonsense solemnly put forward about the "devastating torrent of Indian babies" in a country whose population increase lags behind Britain. In Chapter 4 there is squarely given the contrast between two worlds, socialism in the U.S.S.R. and imperialism in India over two decades, together with a particular contrast of the Central Asian Republics, where almost everything in the past conditions under the Tsar's viceroy was strictly comparable with Hindustan a few hundred miles to the south, and where their present position gives a glimpse of India as it might be.

The need of this first part may be illustrated by the British reader from his own experience. To every school-child the story of the "Black Hole of Calcutta" as the origin and justification of British rule in India, is nearly as familiar as the Norman Conquest, while it is not one in ten thousand who would know of the Moplah death train of 1921. But the "Black

Hole" never occurred. It is a myth, an invented war-atrocity, a lie which does not take on any aspect of truth by its repetition for over a century and half or by being taught to little children.

The atrocious suffocation of the Moplah prisoners of British imperialism, on the other hand, is something that did take place, and less than 20 years ago: but it finds no mention in the school-books. Even when Holwell's monument commemorating the imaginary "Black Hole" was removed two months ago by the Bengal Government from a main thoroughfare of Calcutta because it "offended the susceptibilities" of the inhabitants. *The Times* left it to be inferred that the people of Bengal were unduly sensitive about an episode in their own history and no hint was given that British rule in India came with a lie, or that it was the British who should have felt shame.

In Part II, *British Rule in India*, an historical analysis reveals the secret of Indian poverty; and therewith discusses the reason for the eighteenth- and nineteenth-century primacy of British capitalism and the course of ruling class politics. An examination of the fertile thoughts of Marx on India is followed by a statement of the stages of exploitation from the policy of plunder under John Company to the exploitation of a market for goods with the industrial devastation of Hindustan and from that to the present stage of finance capital, whose stranglehold is expressed in constitutional form in the Government of India Act of 1935. A hundred facts refute the "industrialisation" fallacy. The argument goes deep and the reader may understand from it not only the complex that is India-England but the whole question of imperialism and the subject peoples, can see wider horizons and come to grasp the last century and a half of world history. *British Rule in India* confirms the Communist International thesis on the National and Colonial question.

Of particular importance for the British reader is the exposition in Part III of the *Basic Problem of India—the Agrarian Problem*. Here is not only a clear statement of the process of growing agrarian crisis: the over-pressure of the population on agriculture, due to the continuing "deindustrialisation" of the Indian colony; the stagnation and deterioration of agriculture; the land-hunger of the peasantry, with dwarfish, fragmented and ever-smaller holdings; the whole falling more and more into the maw of absentee landlords; the crushing burden of debt; the expropriation of the peasantry. These developments which have gone on with the remorseless movement of a natural process, which the imperialist rulers of India cannot end without ending their own rule, are now shown to have increased their speed in recent years. Twenty years ago the landless peasants were reckoned at one-fifth of the whole: to-day at *one-half.* Out of this abyss there is no rescue save in the shape of Agrarian Revolution; and Chapter 9 ("The Burdens on the Peasantry") in its closing sentences sounds the prelude to Agrarian Revolution:

> "Carlyle described the situation of the French peasantry on the eve of the Great Revolution in a famous passage:
>
>> The widow is gathering nettles for her children's dinner: a perfumed seigneur, delicately lunging in the *Oeil de Boeuf,* has an alchemy whereby he will extract from her the third nettle, and name it Rent and Law.

A more mysterious alchemy has been achieved to-day in British India. "One nettle is left for the peasant; two nettles are gathered for the seigneur."

Parts II and III, showing the two axes of change in India, the national struggle for liberation from British rule and the oncoming of Agrarian Revolution, give the basis for Part IV, *The Indian People in Movement* (the rise of Indian Nationalism, the three stages of national struggle, and the rise of Labour and

Socialism) and Part V, *The Battleground in India To-day*. To discuss these two parts together with the conclusions in Part VI would require a full treatment in relation to the new developments in India, and the present world situation. Enough has been said to indicate the scope of "India To-day", which becomes the indispensable equipment of every revolutionary. For no one who sees the need of a social transformation can afford to neglect the study of this book or fail to gain from its passion of revolutionary thought an understanding and a stimulus for action.

R. PAGE ARNOT

A Short History of the Russian Revolution

From 1905 to 1937

A Short History of the Russian
Revolution: From 1905 to 1937

A succinct but detailed overview
of the October Revolution and its
development.

156 Pages – 8.5" x 5.5" Paperback

Also available from the publisher:

There Are No Aryans – Robin Page Arnot

Ethics of Socialism - Ernest Belfort Bax

Twenty Years in Underground Russia – Cecilia Bobrovskaya

The Decline of American Capitalism – Lewis Corey

www.PrismKeyPress.com